ANTIQUE PEWTER

OF THE BRITISH ISLES

*A brief survey of what has been made in
pewter in England and the British Isles, from
the time of Queen Elizabeth I to the reign of
Queen Victoria*

RONALD F. MICHAELIS

DOVER PUBLICATIONS, INC.
NEW YORK

Published in Canada by General Publishing Company, Ltd., 30 Lesmill Road, Don Mills, Toronto, Ontario.
Published in the United Kingdom by Constable and Company, Ltd., 10 Orange Street, London WC 2.

This Dover edition, first published in 1971, is an unabridged republication, with minor corrections, of the work originally published by G. Bell and Sons, Ltd., London, in 1955. A new Preface has been written specially for the present edition by the author.

International Standard Book Number: 0-486-22706-5
Library of Congress Catalog Card Number: 74-138387

Manufactured in the United States of America
Dover Publications, Inc.
180 Varick Street
New York, N.Y. 10014

PREFACE TO THE DOVER EDITION

It SEEMS to be a regular practice in the production of a new edition of any work for the author, or some other fit person, to say a few words on the reasons for the venture, and so it is, perhaps, appropriate for me to state, briefly, those which activated me. That the original volume was well received in virtually all European countries, and in all English-speaking nations elsewhere, has been established by the shoals of letters received during the first three or four years after its appearance. Some of these were from persons who had never owned a piece of antique pewterware in their lives, but who had been stimulated to learn more about the craft which had been able to produce such aesthetic examples as were illustrated or described herein, whilst others were from collectors—some of quite long standing—who admitted to a revival of interest and a stimulation to their acquisitive instincts, by virtue of the new light which, they claimed, now illuminated the dim paths they had formerly traversed. A host of new friends resulted from this correspondence, and I am pleased to record that many of those in the first category have now joined the ranks of the converted.

The first edition of this book went rapidly out of print, and has, in consequence, been unavailable except for the limited number of copies on loan from public libraries, or for the occasional volume which turns up on the shelves of a second-hand bookshop (at an inflated price). My concern, therefore, was to be able to satisfy all those later entrants to the pewter-collecting realm who, even today, write to me asking for a copy in the mistaken belief that I might have an unlimited supply.

For my own protection, then, and to save my hand from perpetual writers' cramp, I can now leave it to the publishers and the book trade to tend to their needs!

This book, whether thought to be good, bad or indifferent, has been in popular demand in the United States of America, and it is appropriate that the new edition should be produced there, where there are, in fact, many more collectors of British pewterware than there could possibly be in Great Britain. The book should, however, through normal trade channels, be just as easily obtainable on both sides of the Atlantic.

In casting an eye over the original text I can find little to add unless it be to extend into greater detail on matters already touched upon in brief, but this would take the project out of its concept as a popularly priced handbook, and again have the undesirable effect of pricing it outside the range of the average new collector, so no changes have been made in the text, other than the correction of the few (almost inevitable) printer's errors which have been brought to my notice. The illustrations are, with but a few exceptions, those which adorned the first edition, and have been substituted only in those cases where the originals were no longer available; in every case, however, care has been taken to illustrate good, comparable examples. The bibliographies given at the end of each chapter, and at the end of the book itself, have been augmented by the addition of a few items published since 1955, and should thus help the reader who desires to pursue a wider field of study.

1971   R. F. M.

PREFACE TO THE FIRST EDITION

IT IS just over a quarter of a century since the publication of the last major treatise on the subject of pewterers, their marks, and the wares they produced in the British Isles and, with the exception of a small booklet produced by the editor of one of the foremost antique journals, nothing new on the subject has been printed in book form in England in that period.

True there have been revisions and reprints of one or two older works, and articles on specialized aspects of pewter collecting have appeared in periodicals from time to time, but it is thought that present-day collectors of pewter, and some who, though not yet having joined the ranks, have acquired and come to admire a piece or so, might appreciate a modern book on their chosen pastime.

If this book helps them to a fuller knowledge and appreciation of their treasures the task will be counted well worth while.

In this volume I have attempted to cover as much new ground as is possible within the confines of a moderately-priced handbook, and I have tried to avoid repetition of much of the history of the craft, and details of the alloys used by the old craftsmen—such matters have been very fully dealt with in Welch's *History of the Worshipful Company of Pewterers*, and in other works.

Whilst it may be possible, in some instances, to amplify details of the workings of the 'Mysterie' in London and elsewhere, it seems to me that that can best be done on some other occasion, in a volume confined to the historical aspects, rather than in this book, which is intended to cover the actual hobby of *collecting*.

It is hoped that, in course of time, this volume may come to be looked upon as a real handbook in every sense of the word, both for the beginner searching for knowledge and guidance, and for the more advanced collector as a reference book.

In many respects our knowledge of the early pewterers and their wares, before the beginning of the 17th century, is very meagre, and much of our information is conjectural, but by the selective extraction and analysis of relevant entries in the London Pewterers' Company records it has been possible, in many instances, to make suggestions which may help to identify some early pewterware which, up to the moment, has defied chronological classification.

My grateful thanks are due to the many collectors who have kindly allowed me to make use of photographs of items from their collections of pewter, and to the Directors of Museums, and the other Authorities who have supplied information or illustrations of certain rare pieces. In particular my thanks are due to the Comptroller of the Lord Chamberlain's Office for permission to examine and illustrate the two Elizabethan plates at Hampton Court Palace (shown in Fig. 17).

The source of all borrowed photographs has been acknowledged beneath the illustrations themselves, but where no source is mentioned I have drawn upon my own collection for the specimens required to amplify a particular point or subject.

In conclusion due acknowledgement is made to the late Charles Welch, the author of the published *History of the Worshipful Company of Pewterers, of London,* from which work I have drawn so extensively in this book, and to several Past Masters, and to the Clerk of the Worshipful Company, for allowing these extracts to be used.

R. F. M.

CONTENTS

LIST OF ILLUSTRATIONS

The Line Drawings

The Photographs

CHAPTER ONE

HISTORY AND GENERAL

To ASSIST ONE to a full understanding of the changes in fashion, quality and workmanship of pewterware which have taken place during the long period in which it was an essential and welcome adjunct to practically every home, it is necessary to have, at least, a brief look at the historical background of the craft itself.

Our museums can show specimens of Roman pewter, excavated in England, and there is no reason to doubt that pewterware was actually made in this country by the Roman legions, particularly as all the essential ingredients for its manufacture were readily available. Prior to the Roman invasion tin from Cornwall was mined and exported to Rome, via Gaul overland, and also by ship, and the invaders were already proficient in the uses to which it could be put. In fact Mr. W. R. Lethaby in his *Lead Work* says of tin and lead: 'These two metals made the early fame of Britain; they brought here the Phoenician traders and had doubtless much to do with the Roman occupation of this distant island'.[1]

Harrison, too, in his *Description of England* says: 'Tin and lead, metals which Strabo noteth in his time to be carried into Marseilles from hence, as Diodorus also confirmeth, are very plentiful with us, the one in Cornwall, Devonshire, and elsewhere in the North, and the other in Derbyshire, Weredale and sundry places of this island'.[2]

Pewter is a term used loosely today to include Britannia Metal and all alloys of that nature, irrespective of the amount of tin content, but in ancient times the term 'fine pewter' really meant an alloy of definite and recognizable proportions

[1] Macmillan & Co., London, 1893, p. 5.   [2] op. cit.

I

of tin and copper, and was the metal from which such things as plates, dishes, saucers and other flat ware were made. A lesser alloy known as 'lay' (or ley), to which a proportion of lead was introduced, could be used for hollow vessels such as measures, tankards, candlesticks and shaped objects which, by virtue of their shape, could withstand rough usage without the same risk of serious damage.

A poorer quality of alloy was used for candle moulds, stills, and commercial objects which were fashioned much more clumsily, and did not have to bear the brunt of continual handling and scouring, and for toys, buttons and smaller articles not made for strenuous use or long service.

The earliest written record of an organization for the regulation of the pewter craft in England is of the year 1348, when the pewterers of London petitioned the Mayor and Aldermen of the City for ordinances framed for the protection of the workmen from fraud and unfair competition, and to ensure that a high standard of workmanship and an adequate quality of metal should be maintained thenceforth.

The draft petition was duly approved and ordered to be entered in the City books. This document, originally transcribed in Latin and Norman French, as was the ancient custom, remains in the City archives; and a copy, in quaint early English, is preserved among the records of the Worshipful Company of Pewterers of London.

Mr. H. T. Riley in his *Memorials of London* gives a translation in modern English, which version is used here as being the more easily readable.[1]

ORDINANCES OF THE PEWTERERS,
22 EDWARD III, A.D. 1348

'In the first place—seeing that the trade of pewtery is founded upon certain matters and metals, such as copper, tin and lead, in due proportions: of which three metals they make

[1] 1868, pp. 241-4.

vessels, that is to say pots, salers (salt-cellars), porringers (esquelles), platters, and other things by good folks bespoken: the which things cannot be made without good knowledge of the pewterer, expert and cunning in the craft; (seeing that so many persons not knowing the right alloys, nor yet the mixtures or the right rules of the trade, do work and make vessels and other things not in due manner, to the damage of the people, and to the scandal of the trade, therefore the good folk of the trade do pray that it may be ordained that three or four of the most true and cunning in the craft be chosen to oversee the alloys and workmanship aforesaid: and that by their examination and assay amendment may speedily be made where default has been committed. And if any one shall be found rebellious against the Wardens and Assayers, the default may be sent, with the name of the rebellious offender, unto the Mayor and Aldermen: and that by them he may be adjudged upon, in presence of the good folk of the trade, who have found such default.

'And be it understood, that all manner of vessels of pewter such as porringers, saucers, platters, chargers, pitchers square, and cruets squared, and chrismatories, and other things that are made square or cistils (ribbed), shall be made of fine pewter, with the proportion of *copper* to the tin, as much as of its own nature, it will take. And all other things that are wrought by the trade, such as pots rounded, cruets rounded, and candlesticks and other rounded vessels . . . to be wrought of tin alloyed with lead in reasonable proportions. And the proportions of the alloy are to one hundredweight of tin 22 lb. of lead: and these are always called "vessels of pewter" (vessele desteym).

'Also that no person shall intermeddle with the craft aforesaid, if he be not sworn before the good folk of the craft, truly to work according to the points ordained: such as one who has been an apprentice, or otherwise a lawful workman known and tried among them. And that no one shall receive an apprentice against the usage of the City. And those who shall be admitted therein are to be enrolled according to the usage of the City.

'Also that no person, nor stranger, shall make or bring such manner of vessel of pewter into the City for sale, or offer it for sale before that the material has been assayed, on peril of forfeiture of wares. And if the material be allowable upon assay by the Wardens made, then let the goods be sold for such as they are, and not otherwise. And that no one of the craft shall work privily in secret places vessels of lead, or of false alloy, for to sell out of the City at fairs or markets, to the scandal of the City, and the damage and scandal of the good folk of the craft: but let the things be shown, that shall be so sent to sell without the City, to the Wardens of the trade before they go out of the same, and by them let the things be assayed. And that no one shall do any work in the trade if he will not answer for his workmanship, upon the assay of his work, in whosesoever hands it be found. And if any one shall be found from henceforth carrying such wares for sale to fairs or to markets or elsewhere in the Kingdom before it has been assayed, and, before the Mayor and Aldermen, shall be convicted thereof, let him have his punishment at their discretion, according to his offence, when he shall be so convicted at the suit of the good folk of his trade.

'Also, if any one shall be found doing damage to his master, whether apprentice or journeyman, privily in the way of theft under the value of tenpence; the first time, let amends be made unto the master by him or by his surety in the craft; and if he offend a second time, let his punishment be inflicted by award of the craft; and if he offend a third time, let him be put out of the craft.

'Also, as to those of the trade who shall be found working otherwise than is before set forth, and upon assay shall be found guilty; upon the first default let them lose the material so wrought; upon the second default let them lose the material and suffer punishment at the discretion of the Mayor and Aldermen; and if a third time they shall be found offending, let them forswear the craft for evermore.

'And also, the good folk of the craft have agreed that no one shall be so daring as to work at night upon articles of pewter; seeing that they have regard among themselves to the fact that the sight is not so profitable by night, or so certain, as by day, to the common profit.

'And also, that if any one of the said craft shall be found in default in any of the points aforesaid, he shall pay 40 pence for the first default; for the second default 6s. 8d.; and on the third, let it be done with him at the discretion of the Mayor and the Aldermen; and of these payments let there be given one half to the Chamber, to maintain the points aforesaid, and the other half to the Wardens of the said craft, for their trouble and their expenses.

'And that no one of the trade, great or small, shall take away the journeyman of another man, against the assent and will of his first master, before he shall have fully served his term, according to the covenant made between them, and before the said journeyman shall have made amends to his master for the offences and misprisons committed against him (if he has in any way so offended or misprised), at the discretion of the Wardens of their craft; and whosoever shall do to the contrary of this ordinance, let such person have his punishment at the discretion of the Mayor and Aldermen.

'Also, that no one of the said craft, great or small, shall be so daring as to receive any workman of the craft if he have not been an apprentice, or if he be not a good workman, and one who can have the testimony of his master or of good neighbours of good condition; and can show that well and truly he has served his master for the time assigned between them.'

The careful composition of these ordinances and the mention of 'Wardens of the craft' clearly imply the existence of a

Guild, in one form or another, before 1348, although no record of such a corporation is known to exist. It is, however, abundantly clear from the archives of the Worshipful Company of Pewterers that the Craft, or Fellowship, of Pewterers became increasingly active from that date onwards, but it was not until 1473, in the reign of Edward IV, that the craft received its first Charter, and was thus able to take its rightful place among the City Livery Companies.

Besides the legal benefits of incorporation thus secured the Company was granted the important 'Right of Search' for false wares, not only within the City, but in the suburbs and throughout all England, and the King's officers were enjoined to give them every possible assistance for their purpose.

The Charter was, thus, made known in country districts, and led many provincial pewterers to join the ranks of the London Company.

Whereas, in London, the pewterers, being sufficiently numerous, were able to form into a Company by themselves, this was not possible in country districts, and local pewterers more commonly associated themselves with other trades in common guilds.

In London the Company now took steps to provide itself with a Hall, and Lime Street, off Fenchurch Street, was eventually settled upon as a suitable site. The building of the Hall appears to have commenced in or about the year 1475, and took twenty years to complete.

Inventories of the contents of various apartments of the Hall are extant, and there is no doubt that the building itself was well worthy of the Company. The original Hall was destroyed in the Great Fire in 1666, but was speedily rebuilt and, by the end of the year 1667, the Company took possession of the new building.

We have records of the Pewterers' Guild of York, whose ordinances date from 1419, and follow the same general lines as those of the London Company. Another early guild, confined exclusively to pewterers, was ordained in Bristol in 1456, and here again its rules require adherence to the principles set up in London and York.

From this time onwards we find Guilds of Hammermen, or Smiths, being incorporated at various trading centres in both England and Scotland. The Edinburgh Guild of Hammermen was incorporated in 1496, and during the 16th century Scottish hammermen's guilds were formed at St. Andrews, Perth, Aberdeen and Dundee, with Stirling and Glasgow in 1605 and 1648 respectively.

No specific *pewterers'* guilds have been traced in Ireland, although it is evident that the pewterers of Dublin, Cork and Youghal were embodied in the Smiths' Guilds which operated in those towns.

The main pewtering centres were, therefore, London, York, Bristol and Edinburgh, with places like King's Lynn, Ludlow, Newcastle-upon-Tyne and Kingston-upon-Hull following closely behind. This 'short list' does not, by any means, exhaust the schedule of towns in which local guilds were formed. Groups of pewterers are known to have operated in such places as Barnstaple in Devon, Wigan in Lancashire, and in Gloucester and Hereford, and in these smaller centres they affiliated themselves with other trades in the area.

It is not proposed to go into detail here as to the ordinances and working of these individual centres, but any reader, wishing to study the matter more closely cannot do better than refer to the books and articles mentioned in the Bibliography.

In 1503 was made the first compulsory enactment in London for the affixing of the makers' marks, or touches, upon all vessels made by them.

Such a practice was, however, in use, though not compulsorily, for many years previous to the Act. Pewterers making hollow-ware were enjoined to 'mark the same wares with the several marks of their own to the intent that the makers of

such wares shall avow them . . ., and that all and every of
such wares not sufficiently made and wrought, and not
marked as abovementioned, found in possession of the same
maker or seller to be forfeited.'[1]

'Forfeits', or seizures of false wares (i.e. poor quality of
metal, or badly wrought goods), were frequent, and Welch's
History of the Pewterers' Company teems with instances on
record.

The London Company made good use of its privileges,
granted by the Charter of 1473, to send members to search
in the workshops and on fair stalls, and in all places where
pewter was being made or sold.

The fines imposed on defaulters, and the amounts received
for the base metal in the forfeited ware, helped to pay the
expenses of the searchers who, in the year 1474–5 alone, went
as far afield as Norfolk, Suffolk, Essex, Yorkshire, Derbyshire,
Somersetshire and the West Country. Besides the detection
and seizure of false and dishonest ware these searches resulted in
the enrolment of many country pewterers as brethren of the
London Company; these men were, doubtless, also members
of the local guilds or Associations, but they would have found
it beneficial to keep in close touch with London.

It is this close link between the Guilds and the Pewterers'
Company which ensured almost a uniform quality of metal
being used for each class of wares, irrespective of where they
were made, and this would have had much to do with the
uniformity in shape of vessels for specific purposes.

We shall see, as particular classes of pewterware are discussed, how some styles—once developed—came to be adopted
by both town and country pewterers, however far afield from
each other they may have worked.

The quality of the metal to be used for individual types of
ware varied slightly from time to time—we have seen that, in
1348, flat-ware, i.e. plates, dishes, porringers and such like

[1] 19 Henry VII, Cap. 6.

articles, were to be made of 'fine pewter', with the proportion of copper to tin 'as much as of its own nature it will take'.[1]

All other things that are *wrought* by the trade, such as rounded pots, cruets, candlesticks, etc., were to be made of tin alloyed with lead 'in reasonable proportions'.

The proportions laid down at that time were 22 lbs of lead to each hundredweight of tin.[2] This latter is practically what later came to be known as 'lay' (or 'Ley') metal.

The above two alloys remained more or less standard for flat-ware and hollow-ware respectively, until towards the end of the 17th century, when new classifications were laid down.

In the Charter of 1473 mention is made only of a Master and two Wardens as being responsible for the government of the Craft, but in 1560 all past Masters and Wardens were appointed to sit in deliberation of the Company's affairs, and thus was born the Court of Assistants. In addition to dealing with normal business the Court held indisputable control over every member of the Company, and adjudicated in all disputes between individual members.

Fines for the usage of bad metal or workmanship were impartially imposed upon all offenders, not excepting Master or Wardens, where their actions warranted punishment. If money could not be obtained the Company distrained on tools, stock or even dress.

An offender was sometimes (if a Liveryman) 'deprived of his hood', thus losing the privileges accorded to members of the Livery.

To explain this degradation it will be necessary to review briefly how a pewterer commenced his career. It was the normal practice for a boy to be apprenticed for a period of years (usually seven, but sometimes longer), and, in due

---

[1] Welch gives 'brass' (see Vol. I, p. 3). The amount of brass (copper) which can be absorbed is approximately 26 lbs to 112 lbs of tin (see Massé's *Pewter Plate*, 2nd Edition, p. 19).

[2] Welch gives 26 lbs lead (see Vol. I, p. 3).

course, having served his time, to be presented by his erstwhile master to the Court for examination of his qualifications. Assuming that his master's report on his workmanship and behaviour was favourable, the Court would make the boy 'free' of his apprenticeship, and swear him in as a Freeman of the Company.   The Court's examination sometimes included the submission of a 'proof piece' of the apprentice's own making.[1]

Having obtained his Freedom, the young man could then continue to work for his former master, or could change his employer at will, but he could not set up in business for himself until he had acquired a certain amount of capital and attained a definite standard of skill.   He might then be granted 'leave to open shop, and strike his touch'.

Livery (or Clothing) was awarded to a competent Freeman, usually only after some years' active working on his own account; many pewterers never took livery at all.   However, assuming that our pewterer follows the normal process and, in due course, goes on the livery, he is then eligible for election to the position of Steward with its entitlement to sit on the Court of Assistants, and later to accept the positions of Renter (or Lower) Warden, Upper Warden, and finally Master of the Company, respectively.

By no means all of those who accepted livery continued into the successive offices.   Many reasons may have accounted for their refusal of office, for example, a pewterer may have plied his trade in a country area far removed from London, and he would, thereby, have found it difficult to come continually to London for meetings of the Court, or he may have been in too poor circumstances to bear the costs of the office, which— needless to say—necessitated duties which would take him away from his own work.

In any event, there was in force a system of 'fines', or forfeits, payable by those refusing office, and there are many

[1] Welch, Vol. II, p. 77.

records of pewterers having availed themselves of the opportunity of refusal.

It was customary for every working pewterer to strike his touch upon his wares, and for this to have had any real value it is obvious that an impression of the mark, and a record of its owner, must have been lodged at the Hall, for reference.   The first mention of a 'touchplate' (i.e. a panel of metal, probably pewter, bearing impressions of makers' marks) appears in an inventory of the Company's goods in 1550, where is the entry 'a table of pewter with every mans' mark thereon'. How long this 'table' had been in existence, and whether it included more than one touchplate, will probably never now be known, for all such records are presumed to have perished in the Great Fire of 1666, when the Hall itself was destroyed.

The touchplates preserved by the Pewterers' Company are five in number, and contain a large number of the touches with which pewterers were compelled to mark their wares. These marks, incomplete though they are, are of the greatest interest to the serious collector.   Of these five plates, the earliest was purchased in the year 1667-8, and was brought into use shortly afterwards, and existing pewterers who had, undoubtedly, struck their touches on one or another of the lost plates, were invited to re-strike them on the new plate.

Some of these restruck touches are dated, one being as early as 1640, and some others, though undated, are even earlier.

Most of the restruck touches come within the first 140 on the first plate, and after that the chronological sequence of striking by Freemen who were given leave to open shop is followed almost without a break.   The few exceptions to this sequence must be attributed to the fact that some of the pre-Fire pewterers were unable to attend at Pewterers' Hall immediately for the purpose of making their mark anew.

Towards the end of the 17th century, probably because of the installation of local guilds, the country pewterers began to rebel against supervision by the London Company, and because of frequent legal disputes which made visits unprofitable, the Company became lax in its control of the country trade, with the result that much country pewter became rapidly inferior.

In 1726-7 Bristol pewterers were the subject of a letter written from Philadelphia, complaining of the bad work sent from that town, and in 1728-9 many more complaints were received by the Company, of the poor quality of pewterware from Bristol.[1]

In addition to bad workmanship in provincial areas, there were many instances of country pewterers striking the words 'LONDON' or 'MADE IN LONDON' on their wares, without permission and contrary to Parliamentary decree.

It will be seen that, by this time, the London Company had ceased to be recognized as the governing body of the craft outside London. In London, itself, and in the home counties, however, the Company still maintained a rigid control, which continued until, at least, the middle of the 18th century, and it is for this reason that the term 'London Made' pewter has come to be recognized as the Hallmark of Quality the world over.

Shapes and styles of certain types of pewterware were not left to the whim of individual pewterers, but once satisfactory styles were evolved and had become customary, the Company took strong measures to enforce their uniformity, and on more than one occasion issued decrees laying down in detail the specific weight of each standard item, and the quality of metal from which it was to be made.

In the chapters dealing with each class of ware references will occasionally be made to these decrees, and we shall see how they assist in dating many early specimens of pewterware fairly closely.

Little more need be said here of the craft itself, or of its control of the trade. Readers who desire to make a more

1 Welch, Vol. II, p. 186.

detailed study will need to have reference to the already published matter in such books as appear in the Bibliography at the end of this book, and in the articles below.

BIBLIOGRAPHY

COTTERELL, HOWARD H.: 'The Pewterers of Newcastle upon Tyne', in *Antique Collector*, November, 1935.

COTTERELL, HOWARD H., and CHURCHER, WALTER: 'An Old English Provincial Trade Guild', in *Antiques* (U.S.A.), September, 1926.

MICHAELIS, RONALD F.: 'Some Light on Provincial Pewterers': Part I, *Apollo Magazine*, March, 1946; Part II, 'Metalmen of Gloucester', *Apollo*, May, 1946; Part III, 'A Company of Smiths, of Hereford', *Apollo*, September, 1946.

SHELLEY, ROLAND J. A.: 'Brief Notes on the Wigan Pewterers', a paper read before the Society of Pewter Collectors. (Reprinted for the *Wigan Observer*.) 25th January, 1936.

—— 'Wigan and Liverpool Pewterers', a paper read before the Historic Society of Lancashire and Cheshire, at Liverpool, April, 1945. (Published privately.)

CHAPTER TWO

PLATES, DISHES AND CHARGERS

THE ORDINANCES OF 1348 laid down that dishes, saucers, plates, chargers, square chrismatories 'and other things they make square' should be made of fine pewter, of a standard of metal containing tin with as much copper (or brass) as could be absorbed with it.

The copper content has been worked out to approximate to about 26 lbs of copper to 112 lbs of tin. This ensured a high grade metal which would stand up to constant handling and scouring.

The Company records abound with instances of pewterers who, either wilfully or accidentally, had made ware of metal of poorer quality than the standard (or 'assay') laid down by the Hall, and strong measures were taken against offenders; in the first instance this usually amounted to confiscation of the goods in question, and the imposition of a small fine, but for frequent or persistent lapses, even imprisonment or expulsion from the Company could result.

We have, today, become accustomed to class most flat-ware into the following three categories, viz.: *Plates,* if of normal shallow type, and if not larger than about 10 inches in diameter; *Dishes,* if between 10 and 18 inches; and *Chargers* for those of about 18 inches and over. There has been no hard-and-fast-rule, and most collectors have pleased themselves in the terms they use.

Difficulty arises, however, when one comes across references to pewterware in early wills and inventories, and such terms as 'Sallier', 'Voyder', 'Dobeler' and 'Trencher' appear. How, then, can one correlate these with the titles we use today?

In this chapter some attempt will be made to clarify the

position and, with this object, all relevant entries relating to platters and chargers, etc., in the published history of the Pewterers' Company have been extracted and sifted.

Needless to say, many of the earliest references will be to types which we may never be fortunate enough to find, but as the history draws on towards the close of the 16th century we shall find types which, it is hoped, will emerge as recognizable styles although their descriptions in the language of the period may not agree with those by which we know them today.

It is fortunate that in 1438 a table of weights for most of the pewterware in vogue at that time was compiled, and the following extracted list has especial significance:

Chargers

Chargeours of the largest size to weigh 7 lbs per piece.
Chargeours, the next greatest to weigh 5 lbs per piece.
Middel Chargeours to weigh 3¼ lbs per piece.
Small hollow chargeours to weigh 2¾ lbs per piece.

Platters

Platters of the largest size, to weigh 30 lbs. per doz. 2½ lbs each.
Platters of the next size to weigh 27 lbs. doz. 2¼ lbs each.
Middel platters to weigh 24 lbs. doz. 2 lbs each.
Small middel platters to weigh 22 lbs. doz. 1 lb. 13¼ oz. each approx.

Dishes

[1]Dishes of the largest size to weigh 18 lbs. doz. 1½ lbs. each.
Middel dishes to weigh 14 lbs. doz. 1 lb. 2¾ oz each.
King's dishes to weigh 16 lbs. approx. 1 lb. 5¼ oz each.
Small dishes to weigh 12 lbs. doz. 1 lb each.
Hollow dishes to weigh 11 lbs. doz. 14¾ oz each.
Small hollow dishes to weigh 10 lbs. doz. 13¼ oz each.

Saucers

Saucers of the largest size to weigh 9 lbs. doz. 12 oz each.
Middel size to weigh 8 lbs. doz. approx. 10¾ oz each.
Next to the middel size to weigh 6 lbs. doz. 12 oz each.
[2]Small saucers to weigh 4 lbs. doz. 5¼ oz each.

---

[1] Called Trenchers in 1533. (Welch, 1, 194.)
[2] These were later, in 1563, called Petty Sawcers. (Welch, 1, 247.)

[1]*Galey dishes and Galey saucers*

    Greatest Galey dyshes and Galey saucers, 12 lbs. per doz.

    14 dishes and 14 saucers of the next Galey mold of the small dishes of Galey and Galey saucers, 12 lbs. for 14 of either.

    'Cardinal's hatte and saucers', 15 lbs. per doz.

    'florentyne dishes', 13 lbs. per doz.

    'florentyne saucers', 13 lbs. per doz.

One other item, which can reasonably be included with plates and dishes, is:

    Small bolles (bowls), 13 lbs. per doz.

At this time it was enacted that all 'counterfete' (i.e. wrought) dishes and chargers should be beaten, or hammered, to ensure hardness.

Firstly it should be noted that the terms 'plates' and 'trenchers' do not appear at all, and, secondly, that one of the largest of the 'platters' weighs 2½ lbs. With this given weight we may judge that the diameter of this particular platter was somewhere in the neighbourhood of 13 inches.

We have ample evidence of the large appetites of 'trenchermen' in the middle ages, and it is reasonable to suppose that a platter (i.e. a plate from which food is *eaten*, as distinct from one from which food is *served*) could reach such ample proportions.

So far as the 15th century is concerned we may thus infer that 'chargers' were serving dishes of more than 13 inches diameter.

'Platters' were *eating plates* of about 13 inches diameter, ranging down to about 8 inches, and saucers (i.e. small plates upon which sauces and spices were served) ranged downwards to about 4 inches in diameter.

It seems likely that the dishes and saucers in use from the early 15th century were made with comparatively wide rims, for it is only in 1521–2 that we find the first mention of dishes

[1] The term is later 'Salydysche' and 'Saly sawcer'. The term 'Galey' is probably a misreading of the MSS. for 'Saley' (salad).

and saucers of narrow rim types. In the Accounts of this year the Auditors ask to be allowed xxv s. to lay out upon 'a narro borded dysche mold; a narro borded saucer molde; and a fyllet sawcyr molde'.[1]

It was the practice of the Company to own and keep moulds of most of the standard types of dishes, etc., and these were loaned to the poorer members of the craft.

An inventory of 1451 lists moulds for some of the types given in the 1438 table.

In the Accounts for 1533–4 appears an item 'for ij doss (dozen) Trenchers, . . . waying xviij lbs. at vj d. per lb. ix s.'.[2]

This, incidentally, is the first mention of the word 'trencher'.

Here we have evidence of 2 dozen *Trenchers* weighing 18 lbs (i.e. 9 lbs per dozen, or 12 oz each) which agrees with the tabled weight of 'Sawcers of the largest size' in 1438. All this does is to establish that the larger saucers, of about 7–8 inches in diameter, were used as eating plates.

New types of chargers, platters and dishes are listed in an inventory of 1537–8, as follows: 'and more in pewter belonging to the hall, viz. iij basons and iij yewars (ewers), vj v lb. chargers bareld; xij iij lb chargers bareld'; and in the same list: 'xviij new fassyond platters and iij new fassyond dyscheys from Nicholas Peake'.[3]

The term 'bareld' used above obviously means 'barrelled', and in 1552–3 the type is clearly quoted as 'barrell bordered'. These were, in all probability, dishes with slightly cupped brims, as distinct from those which were quite flat. Types of early 17th-century dishes are known with such a feature.

Just what were 'new fashioned' platters and dishes is not known, neither can we say what was the type mentioned in the following extract, of 1541–2, which reads: 'Item given to the Speaker of the House of Parliament in reward, xij

---

[1] Welch, Vol. I, p. 105. [3] Welch, Vol. I, p. 140.
[2] Welch, Vol. I, p. 134.

ffrench platters and xij disshes of pewter, waying liij lbs. at v d. per lb. xxiiij s'.*[1]

An inventory of 1550 mentions 'Item in 4 lb. chargers barrelled, Item in 5 lb. chargers', and stock moulds, described as 'New fasshion Hatt mould', and a 'Spyce Plate Mould'. Our old friends, the 'narrow bordered dish mould' and the 'narrow bordered sawcer mould', are also listed.

A 'Cardinal's Hat' dish is mentioned in 1438, and the 'new fashioned hat' mould mentioned above indicates that a similar type of dish, but with some new variation, was still in use some hundred years later. The title 'Cardinal's Hat' is used by present-day collectors to denote a broad-rimmed dish with deep well, thought to resemble the shape of hat worn by a Cardinal.

The Company Accounts for 1551–2 contain an entry which reads: 'Item—paid for a half garnish of new ffrench vessels with doble fyllyts and gravyd, and a dosyn of Spanysh trenchers'.

A 'fillet saucer' mould is mentioned in 1521, and now we have French platters with 'double fillets'.

A filleted plate or saucer is, possibly, one which has a rim with a thin beading round the edge on the underside, cast there for strengthening purposes, such as we find in general use on practically all known plates, dishes and chargers of the 16th and 17th centuries. It is difficult to imagine what 'double filleted' can mean, unless it is a larger and heavier beading than that used formerly.

Spanish trenchers are mentioned for the first time in 1551,[2] and are referred to frequently thereafter, but it is not until 1673–4 that we have any description given by which we can define them.[3] In this year is an entry in the records which

---

* *Note.*—This is bad arithmetic—53 lbs at 5d. per lb should be £1 2s. 1d., not £1 4s.—R.F.M.

[1] Welch, Vol. I, p. 146.   [3] Welch, Vol. II, p. 149.
[2] Welch, Vol. I, p. 171.

tells of one Daniel Mason, who was convened before the Court for making plates 'unbeaten in the pitch or booge' (i.e. the curve which links the well of the plate with the rim). Mason alleged that they were 'Spanish plates, and that they are usually so allowed (to be made)', and that he only made the distinction by the striking of a fillet at the request of the buyer.

The Court considered that the filleted rim might cause them to be confused with 'new fashioned plates' (which required better workmanship), and fined him 20s.

This indicates, firstly, that Spanish plates or trenchers were allowed to be made unbeaten in the booge and with less care and workmanship than others and, secondly, that they were usually made without 'fillets'—fillets being reserved for 'new fashioned plates'.

The mention of Spanish trenchers (in 1551) links with a type of plate or dish which we know today as having been carried in the galleons of the Spanish Armada. Several specimens have been dredged up from the sunken Spanish vessels, and Cotterell illustrates one of them in his *Old Pewter* . . . , plate LII(a), from the de Navarro collection, now in the Fitzwilliam Museum, at Cambridge.

This type could quite feasibly be what was previously known (in 1521 and 1550) as a 'narrow bordered dish'.

In 1563, and again in 1571, reminders were issued by the Company to the trade that 'petty saucers', if not of 'foure pounds weight the dozen or thereabouts' were not to be made or sold, and in 1595 it was enacted that none of the Company 'shall at any time hereafter turn any saucer, but (shall make) only those which shall be beaten with the hammer. . . .' In the following year, however, it was agreed that 'turned saucers may be made, until further notice'.

It was the custom to beat all sadware (i.e. plates, dishes and other flat-ware) to ensure maximum strength, and woe betide any pewterer who was found doing otherwise. One example is that of Daniel Mason, already mentioned, and in

1620 is a record of one Arthur Hodgekis admonished 'for burnysshing of his sadd ware'.

Offences seem to have persisted throughout the years, however, for again (in 1667–8), after certain irregularities in the making of sadware, especially of trencher plates, having been discussed, the Court ordered that 'all trencher plates (except Spanysh) should be beat all over as well Pitch or Bouge as elsewhere', and that they should 'not be suffered to be turned in ye booge or pitch'.[1]

In 1690–1 the Court ordered that 'all Spanysh and other plates that can be beat in the pitch shall be beat in that part as well as in any other parts thereof'.[2] If we are correct in assuming that plates and dishes of the type shown in Fig. 16 are what were then known as 'Spanish trenchers' we have examples in collections today, both 'unbeaten in the booge' and 'beat all over'.

This specimen has a raised beading round the underside edge of the rim, and it is probable that it dates from the early to mid-17th century.

It is a deplorable fact that, despite this multitude of information on mediaeval and later pewterware, and on plates in particular, we are unable to say with certainty which of the various types are the earliest of those which have come down to us.

The London and the Guildhall Museums, to name only two, own between them numerous specimens of small deep-welled plates, or 'sawcers', which have been excavated from sites in or near London, and there can be little doubt that some of them can date back to, at least, the 16th century. Accurate dating is made difficult because, even when maker's marks appear—and this is not always the case—the mark is not recorded elsewhere and the maker is unknown.

In one case only does some possible ray of light seem to emerge, and even in this case the conclusions are somewhat

[1] Welch, Vol. II, p. 135.   [2] Welch, Vol. II, p. 164.

conjectural. Fig. 17 shows a pair of small deep saucers with a rim width of 1⅜ inches; on the front of the rim is stamped a Tudor Rose Crowned, and the initials 'E' and 'R'. The maker's mark of a Crowned Bell is struck on the back. (See drawing.)

These two small saucers are at Hampton Court Palace, and they are, presumably, of the period of (and formerly the property of) Queen Elizabeth I.

There seems little doubt that we can, in this instance, attribute these pieces to a known maker, for the records of 1573-4 tell of a pewterer, Nicholas Jurdeine, who was in dispute with the Master and Wardens over his touch, and he was ordered to *'give up his touch of the Crowned Bell'*.

Nicholas Jurdeine (or Jardein) was a Merchant Taylor who had married the widow of a pewterer, Robert Hustwaite, and continued the trade with his wife. He was made a brother of the Company on 18th September, 1573, although he had not served his apprenticeship in the normal way. He seems to have been quite active in the trade and is mentioned on various occasions between the years 1573 and 1581, sometimes for misdemeanours (possibly due to ignorance of the regulations), and upon occasions when apprentices were bound to him.

Assuming, from the mark, that the Hampton Court saucers were, in fact, made by him, we have additional confirmation of their age in the Royal Cypher punched upon them, and we can vouch for their authenticity as they were excavated in the grounds of the Palace.

Thus, we have the first type which can be dated with any reasonable degree of certainty.

There is another group of early plates which, so far, has defied reliable chronological identification. In Fig. 18 is shown a specimen from a batch of about a dozen which were found together when the foundations of a new wing of Guy's Hospital were being dug in 1899. All of them bear a punched mark on the front of the rim, in the form of a Crowned

Feather, and some, but not all, bear upon the reverse a small maker's mark which could, conceivably be likened to a Bell, although not in any way like that already described.

All of these plates are of approximately similar type—some with bossed centres, and others without boss. Cotterell shows one of these plates in his *Old Pewter* . . ., plate LI(f), from the de Navarro collection (now in the Fitzwilliam Museum, at Cambridge), and further specimens are in the London Museum and Guildhall Museum, and in other private collections.

Another early plate, of a similar type to the former group, is

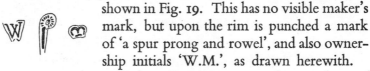

shown in Fig. 19. This has no visible maker's mark, but upon the rim is punched a mark of 'a spur prong and rowel', and also ownership initials 'W.M.', as drawn herewith.

It is not easy to give even an approximate date to plates of this type; it is probable, however, that they can be attributed to 15th- or, at least, early 16th-century pewterers.

The next illustration shows a small broad-rimmed plate, of a type which can be dated fairly accurately to the first half of the 17th century. Many of these plates have been used for ecclesiastical purposes as Patens, or, perhaps, as Flagon stands, and collectors have become accustomed to use the term 'paten' in describing them. Needless to say, it is incorrect to use this appellation unless there is undoubted evidence of their use by the church. Such evidence may sometimes be provided by an engraved inscription, which can identify the plate with a known church.

The paten—for such it is—in Fig. 20 was donated to the church by one 'Samuel Symonds, Gent', and bears an inscription to this effect.

Broad-rimmed dishes, with shallow curved well, and others with bossed centres, can sometimes be found with recognizable marks of mid 17th-century pewterers.

The example shown in Fig. 21 has an exceptionally deep

well, with a centre boss, and bears the mark of a pewterer who re-struck his mark on the new touchplate of the Pewterers' Company in 1667, and, thus, it can be dated with reasonable certainty as of the period *c*.1650–75. An almost identical dish, but with plain deep well, is illustrated and recorded in *The Church Plate of Hampshire* as being (in 1909) in the possession of the Church of St. Mary, Twyford.[1] This type seems to bear all the characteristics of the so-called 'Cardinal's Hat'.

Broad-rimmed dishes, with perfectly plain rims, date from the early 17th century to *c*.1675, and, as time progressed, the width of the rim diminished somewhat, and, from about 1675 onwards, plates and dishes were adorned by a reeded moulding round the edge of the rim. The earliest form of multiple reeding was by incised lines and grooves, made by a cutting tool held against the rim whilst the plate was turning on a lathe.

These can be easily identified because all the lines and grooves must, necessarily, be below the surface, as shown in the drawings of plate rims in Fig. 1.

There is little doubt that such reedings were applied in the first instance in imitation of those on contemporary silver plates, but gradually they came to be adopted as a standard addition on pewter plates and dishes; later moulds were made with the grooves already cut, thus obviating the lathe work. Parts of the reeding on dishes of the later type are found to rise above the normal surface level, as shown.

Plates, of not more than 10 inches in diameter, with multiple reeded rims, are far less numerous than are large dishes of otherwise similar type.

There is a quite distinct group of multiple reeded-edge plates which has a brim very little wider than the reeding itself, and these have become known by the simple title of 'narrow rim plates'. They are usually of a size between 8½ inches and 9½ inches diameter, although, very rarely, one finds a dish, of perhaps 15 inches or so in diameter, similarly reeded.

[1] Rev. P. R. P. Braithwaite, M.A., London, Simpkin Marshall, 1909.

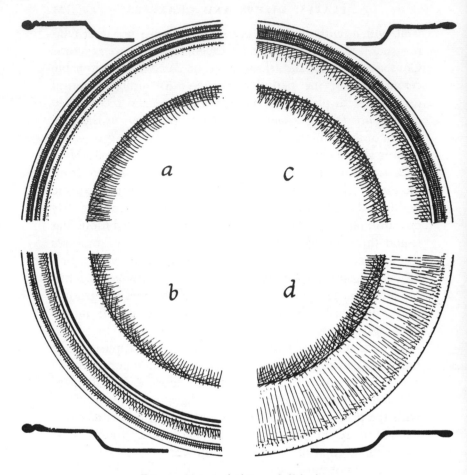

FIG. 1. Types of plate and dish rims

(*a*) Incised multiple reeding, in which all grooves lie below the flat surface, and are gouged out on a lathe. (Late 17th century.)

(*b*) Cast multiple reeding. This type of reeding is cast on at the time the dish is made, and parts stand proud of the surface. (Late 17th century.)

The above two mouldings are usually termed 'triple reedings'.

(*c*) Single reeding; cast in the mould, as (*b*). (Early to mid 18th century.)

(*d*) Plain rim with no surface reeding, but with a thickened moulding on underside. (Mid 18th to early 19th century.)

Fig. 22 shows both plate and dish with similar triple reeding.

Specimens of this type, bearing known makers' marks, have enabled us to date them during the period c.1670–90. From their shape it seems likely that they are the direct evolution of the circular treen platters in use in former times.

Following closely on the heels of the triple-reeded types comes the 'single-reeded' group. All sizes of plates, dishes and chargers were made with one deep groove about a quarter of an inch from the edge of the brim. Plates and dishes, which can date as early as 1690, have been found with this type of reeding, but, in the earlier specimens, the brim itself is slightly less in width than on the 18th-century pieces. Another feature worthy of mention is that the brims are cupped upwards rather more than on former types.

There is very little difference between English and continental plates of this style, and the reader is advised to study the marks closely to distinguish one from another. One sure sign of a continental plate is the incidence of the maker's mark *struck three times*. This does not occur in all foreign specimens, but it does appear frequently. English pewterers did not strike their touch more than twice on one piece, and, more often, only once.

The fashion for single-reeded plates lasted well into the second half of the 18th century, and overlapped, by about forty years, the last main group, which we shall call 'plain rimmed'.

Here there is no facial adornment of reeding, but the narrow raised beading on the underside is slightly more robust than on all earlier types. Plates and dishes (including chargers up to more than 30 inches in diameter) were made in this style, right up to the first quarter of the 19th century, when pewter for normal table purposes seems to have taken its bow. Pottery and porcelain at this time was being produced so cheaply that pewter (which needed much more cleaning and scouring) was relegated to the servants' quarters and, thence, to the attics.

It is interesting to note that a dinner service in this style was produced by a London pewterer, one Thomas Alderson, for the Coronation banquet of George IV.[1] Individual pieces, which bear upon the rim the Royal Cypher 'G. IV R.' engraved in cursive script, and surmounted by a Crown, are occasionally met with in private collections.

There are several other types of English plates which cannot be overlooked, although they never attained the same degree of popularity as did the types already discussed.

In particular there are the five- and six-lobed plates, several types of which are shown in Fig. 23. These are sometimes called 'wavy-edged plates'. This seems to have been a style copied from the Continent, where such plates and dishes were in much more common use. Various English makers, of from c.1750 to about 1775, have produced one or another of these styles, but none to any great extent.

Oval dishes for joints, of both the plain-rimmed type and 'wavy-edge' series, were made to complete the dinner services.

Sexagonal-, octagonal- and decagonal-sided plates and small dishes were made by several makers. These date from about the same period as the 'wavy-edged' styles, but, again, do not seem to have attained any great popularity in their own time.

BIBLIOGRAPHY

COTTERELL, H. H.: 'Old Pewter Plates and Chargers', *Bazaar, Exchange and Mart*, 31st August, 7th and 14th September, 1923.
—— 'Rim Types of Old Pewter Plates', *Connoisseur*, February, 1919.
—— 'Jewish Passover Plates', *Connoisseur*, April, 1928.
—— 'Old Pewter Scale Plates', *Connoisseur*, March, 1931.
—— 'Evolution of the Trencher', *Antiques* (U.S.A.), January, 1930.
—— 'Evolution of the Pewter Plate', *Antique Collector*, October, 1931.
SUTHERLAND GRAEME, A. V.: 'Pewter Rosewater Dishes', *Connoisseur*, June, 1935.
—— 'Pewter Restoration Chargers', *Connoisseur*, June, 1942.
—— 'Some Pewter Plates', *Connoisseur*, December, 1941.

[1] Held at Westminster Hall in July 1821.

CHAPTER THREE

DRINKING VESSELS

ALTHOUGH OUR MUSEUMS possess several specimens of early drinking cups and beakers, which one is tempted to ascribe to the 16th century, or possibly earlier, there is no 'yardstick' by which we can be certain of their period, and we must, therefore, fall back on the Pewterers' Company records for what information they can give, in the hope that some recognizable types will emerge.

The earliest types of pewter vessels used specifically for drinking purposes, mentioned in these records, are of the year 1482, when we find both 'Tanggard potts' and 'Stope potts' (i.e. Stoop or Stoup pots), but it is not possible to say what forms they took at that time.

We have comparatively little in silver of this period to help us in forming any opinion.

In 1489 is a further mention of 'iiij pottes called drynkyng cruses' (which were possibly some form of Costrel, or Pilgrim's Bottle); and 'goblettes of peauter of fflaundres makyng'. These latter were imported goods included in a batch of pewterware which had been seized by the searchers for destruction; and, in the same year, a further mention of 'vj drynkyng pottes with coveryng, called stopes, weying xij lbs.'. The latter entry, at least, establishes that 'stope pots' were lidded vessels.

In the Accounts for 1503–4 appears an item for 'boylyng and burnysshing of ij cuppes'; and in 1535–6 there were seized from a haberdasher '. . . vj gobblets and iiij dozen stone pot heads' (i.e. pewter lids for stone pots). It was customary for haberdashers to retail small pewterware, and references to

their offences in the handling of inferior quality goods appear
frequently in the records.

An inventory of 1537–8 mentions 'xv small drynkyng
potts', and another inventory of 1550 has 'Item—in Stope
pynts, xijs.' and 'Item—in Nuf' (*sic*) (i.e. New Fashioned)
halfe pynts, xiiijs.'.

Beakers are first mentioned in 1595–6, when some beakers
and other pewterware, made by Humfrey Weetwood and
Thomas Cowes, were found to be of 'false' (i.e. inferior) metal;
but it is not until 1612–13 that some definite light begins to
break through the gloom, and we are given some inkling of
the names by which they were known, and their weights.[1]
In this year a large variety of 'tryffles' were listed, and standard
weights were adjudged for the benefit and guidance of
pewterers. This list mentions Beakers, Bowls and Cups,
with their weights, as follows:

Beakers

The greate beakers, wrought, ½-doz. to weigh 4½ lbs.
Greate beaker, plain, ½-doz. to weigh 5½ lbs.
Middle beaker, ½-doz. to weigh 3¼ lbs.
Smale beaker, ½-doz. to weigh 2¾ lbs.
Children's beakers, wrought, ½-doz. to weigh 1½ lbs.
Children's beakers, plain, ½-doz. to weigh 1 lb.

Bowles and Cuppes

The greate Beere bowle, ½-doz. to weigh 6¼ lbs.
Small Beere bowle, ½-doz. to weigh 4¾ lbs.
Large wrought Cuppes, ½-doz. to weigh 3¼ lbs.
Middle French Cupps, ½-doz. to weigh 3 lbs.
Small French Cupps, ½-doz. to weigh 2¼ lbs.
High Wine Cupps, wrought and plain, ½-doz. to weigh 3 lbs.
The Cutt short Cupps, ½-doz. to weigh 3 lbs.

In this same year mention is made of one William Lobb,
who was sent to prison for making beer bowls '30 grains
worse than fine in the foot, and 3 grains worse in the body'.

[1] Welch, Vol. II, p. 61.

So far we have no indication, from pieces within our ken, of what form was taken by these 'beere bowls', but it is likely that the cups were with, at least, one handle, since we know that beakers, as a general rule, are handleless vessels.

The earliest form of the handled cup known in pewter is shown in Fig. 24. Such cups, sometimes with one handle only, are to be found in the Guildhall, London, and Victoria and Albert Museums.

The lines of these cups follow very closely the silver models in vogue in the early to mid-17th century.

The last reference to cups in the Company records seems to be in 1675, when one William Allen was forbidden to use 'soft pale' for soldering his cups. ('Soft pale' is solder of a much poorer quality than the article upon which, in this case, it was used.)

There are, however, two further references to beakers which may, in course of time, prove of use in locating specimens; these are, firstly, in 1622–3 when (among articles seized because of bad workmanship, from Edward Starton) there was 'one great beaker pinte, marked with a starre'. It is of considerable interest for us to know that Starton used the mark of a 'Star', and whilst (so far as is known to the writer) no specimen with this mark has come to light, there is always that possibility.

It was also during this year (1622–3) that searchers found, in the house of some pewter dealers, 'some smallest paynted beakers'.

The term 'paynted' in this instance refers to *gilded* pewter, as is made apparent from a later entry in the records.

This particular offence seems to relate either to children's beakers or to toys.

Pewterers had previously been forbidden to gild any pewter-ware except it be a small gift or trifle not made for sale.

Several early beakers are known, but because of their being unmarked, or because their marks cannot be attributed to any known maker, it is not possible to be precise as to date, but there is good reason to believe that some, at least, are Elizabethan.

There is a small group of beakers, bearing cast ornamentation, including designs and motifs which can be placed fairly certainly as of James I period, which will be dealt with more fully in another chapter. At the present time we are more concerned with shape and style than with ornamentation.

A glance at the photographs of the two early Stuart beakers shown in Figs. 82 and 84 will show an affinity in the foot moulding, and this is a fairly sure way of distinguishing early

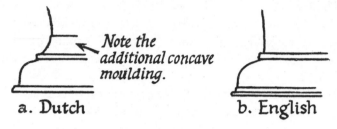

Note the additional concave moulding.

a. Dutch   b. English

FIG. 2. Comparison of Dutch and English beaker foot mouldings.

English beakers from the otherwise similar and contemporary continental examples.

The drawings on this page will, perhaps, illustrate this difference more clearly. The English moulding curves outwards, and is hollow underneath up to the point where it meets the straight side of the vessel. The moulding on Dutch specimens has an added concave moulding above the deep convex foot rim. Elizabethan silver beakers have a foot rim of a style which, so far, has not been found on a pewter example.

Pewter beakers continued to be made throughout the 17th century, and on until c.1840 or so, but, as time progressed, the long and slender form gave place to the more squat types, such as those illustrated in Fig. 25. These are all of ½-pint capacity, and range in date from about 1780 to c.1840. There is abundant evidence that beakers of this type have been frequently used in taverns as drinking vessels and, doubtless, often as measures.

Of those shown, at least five of them bear Excise stampings which indicate that the capacity has been checked by Local Inspectors.

Despite the fact that 'tanggard pots' were mentioned as early as 1482, it is not until the middle of the 17th century that we find examples of tankards which can be dated with any degree of accuracy.

Many types of tankards and 'pots', both with and without covers, are mentioned in the Company records, and it is as well to quote all the available references for the benefit of those who may be able, in time to come, to associate some known pieces with one or another of the given descriptions.

In 1554-5 one William Redman was fined for not placing a touch upon 'vj Bow potts'. In 1557-8 the Court agreed that 'no person from henceforth shall make any tankard potts or hoped (hooped) potts but they shall sother (solder) the same with fine mettall in all places, saving only the setting in of the bottom . . .'.

It is sometimes difficult to draw a distinction between tankards and measures in these early periods; the records are not precise in their descriptions, and it is also probable that the vessels served the dual purpose.

For example, an entry of 1563 refers to an Order that 'as from this day (29th April) no pewterer shall make any barred pottes of pewter, but only thirdendales and half thirdendales'.

It was also ordered that the Keeper of the Standard 'shall not seale any other barred potts from henceforth of any other quantity'.

In the following year an Ordinance confirmed the above order, and it was extended to include 'the pot called the brode (broad) pint, and that no hollow-ware man shall make any potts of just quarts or pints for Ale or beere measures, but only the stope pottell; the greate stope quart; and the great stope pint; and the great stope pint with the brode bottom; the English pottell; the great English quart; the great English pint and none other'.

In 1588 (10th October) it was ordained that there should be no 'tankerd quart potts' made, of less weight than 2½ lbs the piece, but some pewterers had evidently digressed, for at a further meeting on 15th October, 1588, the records state that 'whereas divers of the Company have circumvented in that, to their advantage, they have made tankerd quart pottes at ij lbs the piece; the inconvenience of it being considered it is ordered that, if any of the Company do make the thurrendell tankerd potte at lesse weight than 3 lb; the tankerd quarte at (less than) 2½ lbs; the short potte at (less than) 2 lb, and the longe potte at less than 1 lb, they shall paye for every suche potte fyve shillings for a fine'.

If one reads the above entry in conjunction with a later entry of 1612–13, where weights for various classes of pewterware are given, it will be seen that a 'thurrendale (thurndell, thurdendale)' is a tankard *capacity*, rather than a type of vessel.

In this list we find:

> New fashion thurndell
> New quarts
> New halfe thurndells
> New greate pints
> New small pints
> Hooped thurndells
> Great hooped quarts
> Winchester quarts, with lid
> Winchester pint, with lid
> Winchester quart, without lid
> Winchester pint, without lid
> Long hooped Winchester pints
> Jeayes danske pots

The weights given in the records for some of these items are confusing and are not, therefore, quoted.—R.F.M.

To judge from the sequence of sizes as quoted, there is every indication that a thurndell (or thurdendale) was a measure (or possibly a tankard), holding three pints of liquid; but even if this assumption is correct we have yet to discover an Elizabethan pewter tankard of 3 pints (or, for that matter, of any other) capacity.

The earliest tankards which we can date with any reasonable degree of certainty are flat-topped tankards of the types shown in Fig. 27.

Such tankards are considered to have been made from c.1660, and, with variations, continued in use until c.1700.

During the earlier part of the 17th century, however, the terms 'Danske pott' and 'Ephraim pintes' are found, and the Company records of 10th August, 1638, state 'It is ordered that from henceforth all Danske potts, both with lids and without lids, shall be burnished within', and, in 1667–8, one Charles Richardson got into trouble for his 'Ephraim pintes' which were found to be '2 grains worse than standard'. In 1673 a new table of weights is given, and the few items quoted below may throw a little light on specimens yet to be identified:—

Ephram and other potts:
>Three quarts, 4½ lbs. each
>Two quarts, 3 lbs. 2 oz. each
>Three pint, 2 lbs. 2 oz. each
>Quart, 1 lb. 10 oz. each
>Pint, 1 lb. 2 oz. each
>½-pint, ¾ lb. each

Winchester quart, each 1¼ lbs.
Guiny potts or Tunn pintes, each dozen, 12 lbs. (1 lb. each piece).
Long and short Cann, each, ¾ lb.

New fashioned tankards:
>Great quarte, each, 2½ lbs.
>Small quart, each, 2 lbs.
>four inches, each, 1¾ lbs.
>pint, each, 1½ lbs.
>Ordinary 4 inch. 1 lb. 6 oz.

FIG. 3. A Danish
tankard, of *c.*1675–80.

FIG. 4. A Danish
tankard, by a Kiel
maker, *c.*1695.

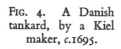

So far no tankard or drinking vessel of any sort can be definitely identified with the terms 'danske' and 'ephraim'; the most likely possibility is that a danske pot is, in fact, a *Danish* pot, or tankard.

Danish tankards of this period were cylindrical bodied and shallow-lidded vessels—not unlike our own flat-lidded Stuart tankards, and the English type may well have been evolved from the Scandinavian.

Figs. 3 and 4 show two Danish tankards of the latter part of the 17th century, for comparison with the English types of a few years later, shown in Fig. 27.

There is every reason to believe that the 'new fashioned tankards' can also be identified with the known English flat-lidded tankards.

Treading upon the heels of the flat-lidded tankards came the types with a domed cover—in fact, pewterers were 'on with the new love, ere off with the old'.

The earlier forms of domed cover had a denticulated frontal serration, similar to that which appeared on some of the flat covers, and the drums were completely plain and unbanded, as formerly. The slight curving, or entasis, which was a feature of the drum of most flat-lidded tankards, is not so pronounced in domed types, and, in some cases, does not appear at all.

It is doubtful if the domed type was used much before 1685, but that it was made in that year is amply proved by the design in a pewterer's touch (*shown hereunder*), which displays a clearly-defined domed tankard, with plain drum, and has incorporated with it the date (16)85.

This mark was struck on the touch-plate in that year, No. 420, and is, thus, fully authenticated.

The frontal projection to the cover disappeared on later examples, and by the turn of the century tankards were made with a single band of

The mark of John Smith, pewterer, from the London touch-plate, No. 420, struck in 1685.

moulding (or fillet) round the centre of the drum, as seen in
Figs. 28 and 29.

Several types of handle variations will be found on flat-
lidded tankards, but none of these became standard upon
domed tankards. For domed tankards pewterers adopted an
entirely new type of handle with a terminal appendage which
can be likened to a ball. Tankards with this handle date
from c.1685 to about 1720. (See Fig. 28.)

A later type of handle terminal, commonly termed 'fish-tail'
(such as may be seen in the examples in Fig. 29), came into
vogue about the year 1710, and continued during the lifetime
of this type of tankard. Covers vary slightly in the height and
style of the dome but, to all intents and purposes, the general
shape persisted until about 1750.

Another type of lidded Georgian tankard has a 'tulip-
shaped' body and is usually surmounted by a domed cover;
the earlier examples of this type bear a single-curved handle
with 'ball' terminal (as on the first of the cylindrical domed-lid
tankards), and the covers are adorned with a 'chairback'
thumbpiece. (See Fig. 26.) In the course of time the thumbpiece changed to one of outline only, and this has become
known as the 'open' thumbpiece.

Tulip-shaped tankards date from about 1730 to 1800; and
after this date comparatively few lidded tankards were
produced.

Isolated examples of late lidless types, to which covers
have been attached at a later date, are found, but they do
not conform to any definite standard design. Last of all
came the covered pots with glass bases, the drums often
engraved with dates and particulars of University Rowing
'Eights' and 'Fours', and were, obviously, either prizes or
trophies for competing teams in the mid-19th century and
later.

In conjunction with the various types of lidded tankards of
the late 17th and early 18th centuries, there were some par-

ticularly pleasant lidless tankards which were quite dissimilar in all respects from their contemporaries.

Specimens of early lidless tankards are shown in Figs. 30 and 31.

A notable feature of most of these tankards is the sharply-tapering 'rake' of the drum; this is accentuated by the slimness of the body in comparison with all lidded tankards of coeval date.

It is not unusual to find punched 'Capacity Seals' (i.e. marks denoting that the capacity has been checked and found correct) bearing the Crowned letters 'W.R.' or 'A.R.'(representing William Rex, or Anne Regina). Upon tankards of these styles and from engraved examples we can date them from c.1675 to c.1730.

From this date onwards to the third quarter of the century covered tankards were obviously the more favoured, for it is a rare circumstance to find a lidless tankard which can be dated between, say, 1730 and 1780. In the 1780's and for the succeeding twenty-five years or so the style principally in vogue was of plain tapering cylindrical form (as in Fig. 32).

At the turn of the century and well on into the Victorian period various changes in style are to be observed, and it is difficult to place succeeding types into any chronological sequence. Fig. 33 shows a variety of lidless tankards which range from c.1835 to c.1850 and some of these styles persist to the present day.

BIBLIOGRAPHY

COTTERELL, H. H.: 'Tavern Pewter', *Antique Collector*, August, 1931.
—— 'Pewter and Mulled Ale', *Antique Collector*, September, 1931.
—— 'Dating the Pewter Tankard', *Connoisseur*, April, 1932.

BISSET, J. S.: 'Scottish Pewter Tankards', *Antique Collector*, September, 1937.

DE NAVARRO, ANTONIO: 'Evolution of the Pewter Tankard': Part I, *Country Life*, 8th September, 1906; Part II, 9th March, 1907.

MINCHIN, CYRIL C.: 'Flagons and Tankards, in Pewter', *Antique Collector*, February, 1952.

SUTHERLAND GRAEME, A. V.: 'Early Pewter Tavern Pots', *Connoisseur*, March, 1941.

—— 'Pewter Tavern Pots', *Country Life*, 28th October, 1954.

CHAPTER FOUR

MEASURES

VESSELS OF TRUE MEASURE have been made in this country probably from time immemorial, but a reference in Welch's *History of the Pewterers' Company* as early as the 29th June, 1351, mentions 'twenty-three measures, called "potels", of false metal (i.e. the greater part of lead) made by John de Hiltone, were seized (for destruction)'. This indicates that even in those early days the craft was rigidly supervised and controlled; and over the next three hundred years these same records cite instances of defaulters in weight or quality and, in many cases, foretell the penalties which will be meted out to offenders.

The first mention of standard weights for certain types of measures occurs in 1438,[1] as follows:

> Square potel, 4 lbs. each
> Square quart, 2½ lbs. each
> Square pint, 1½ lbs. each

and, in 1482,[2] a more comprehensive list is given, which includes:

Normandy pottes	Pottell
	Quarte
	Peingte
Household pottes	Pottell
	Quarte
	Peingte
Measure pottes	Gallon
	Pottell
	Quarte
	Peingte
	Halfe peingte

Stope pottes (no sizes quoted)

---

[1] Welch, Vol. I, p. 12. [2] Welch, Vol. I, p. 57.

As yet, we have no indication of the form or style of any of these types. The earliest pewter measures which have come to light, and which we can be sure are English, are what we know as Baluster Measures. No one has yet been able to say with certainty that these were made prior to the end of the 16th century, but some writers have believed them to date, at least, from the mid-16th century.

This dating has been suggested by the form of a capacity

 mark, or 'seal', impressed on the cover, or elsewhere on the piece itself, which is said to be the mark indicating that the capacity conforms to the standard of Henry VIII. The mark in question is a Crown, beneath which are the letters 'h.R.', as in the accompanying drawing.

Whether the mark originated as suggested is conjectural; there being no reliable evidence to prove the point. It is possible to say, however, that an almost identical mark appears on baluster measures *unquestionably* made much later. That illustrated in Fig. 37, for example, can be dated by the maker's mark as of *c*.1690.

To revert to the mid-16th century records it is interesting to note the steps taken to punish offenders, for, in addition to a fine of £10 'if any member makes or causes to be made any measure potts, commonly called tavern potts, of any lease (less) measure than by the standard appoynted for the same potts, the defaulter shall also stand on the pillory on three lawful Market days according to the order of the Citye'.

In the same year (15th January, 1556) one Robert West was 'sent to the Warde for makyng false measure potts', and, at a later Court (14th June, 1556) it was agreed that 'all suche persones (who) had any potts made by the said Robert West should as well bring a bill of such weight and also the loss sustained by the same'. Here follows a list of eleven known pewterers. By this it would seem that one maker, who specialized in a certain type of ware, would make that ware

for other pewterers.   This assumption is borne out by a table
of charges mentioned in 1482, which specifies the charges to be
levied for casting certain ware for the trade.

In 1612, when weights were standardized for specific types
of vessels, a new title appears for measures as 'Spowt potts'
in the following sizes:[1]

> The pottle, per piece 8¼ lbs.
> quarte, per piece 3 lbs.
> pinte, per piece 2 lbs.
> ½ pint, per piece 1¼ lbs.

The mention of spouts rules out any baluster measures
which we know today, but brings us no nearer to knowledge
of the type indicated.   No spouted measures of this early date
are known to the writer.

By the beginning of the 17th century the importation and
use of earthenware pots for tavern purposes was reaching
alarming proportions, so far as the pewterers were concerned.
There are frequent references to the making of pewter lids
for 'stone potts', and further evidence is forthcoming in 1632,
when the Pewterers' Court moved that a petition should be
preferred to His Majesty's Council to the effect that no
victuallers or others should sell any beer or ale 'but in pewter
potts'.[2]

It is not apparent whether this petition was actually preferred, nor of the outcome, but the pewterers did not let the
matter rest, for in 1649 a further petition was drawn up—
Item 3 reading as follows: 'That all measures for liquid Commodities may be made of such mettle or stuffe as will take the
faire Impression of a seall'.[3]

In the writer's opinion the 'seall' referred to therein is, in
fact, a mark certifying capacity, and is most probably that
already described at the beginning of this chapter.   The
Crowned 'h.R.' mark is certainly more frequently found on

---

[1] Welch, Vol. II, p. 62.   [3] Welch, Vol. II, p. 113.
[2] Welch, Vol. II, p. 90.

measures which one is more inclined to date as of the 17th than of the 16th century.

In fact, a variation of this mark, with capital letters 'H.R.', placed upon either side of the City of London Arms, is found upon measures dating up to, at least, the end of the 18th century.

In 1696, following a petition from the Tin Farmers of Cornwall, a resolution was made by the Committee of the House of Commons 'That for encouraging the consumption of Tin and advancing the price thereof no wine, beer, ale, brandy, rum or other spirits be sold by retail in any Tavern or other public house, but in sealed measures made of pewter'.[1]

In 1702 the Pewterers' Court was informed 'of a greate increase of Muggs made of Earth and a mark impressed thereon, in imitation of Sealed Measures to sell liquid commodities in'[2] and, again in 1708, at a Court of 15th December 'One Mr. Wroth, Clerk of the Markett of the Queen's Household declared that the principall Potters who made Muggs lived within his jurisdiction, and that their muggs, though sealed, were not of full (at least, of uncertain) measure'.[3]

These further references leave us in no doubt as to the meaning of 'sealed measures', and we do, in fact, find frequent examples of a Crowned 'W.R.' capacity mark, and, more rarely, a Crowned 'A.R.', applied in the same manner, and for the same purpose, as the Crowned 'h.R.'.

The reference to the 'Clerk of the Queen's Household' may provide a clue to explain the 'h.R.' mark, about which there has previously been so much controversy. Could this not be intended to represent 'household Rex (or Regina)' or possibly even 'household Royal'? It is difficult, otherwise to reconcile the small letter 'h' with the capital letter 'R' of the earlier marks, and it would certainly explain why the mark is found over so long a period, and so long after the reign of Henry VIII.

---

[1] Welch, Vol. II, p. 168.   [3] Welch, Vol. II, p. 176.
[2] Welch, Vol. II, p. 173.

In 1673–4 (14th April), the Court produced a new table of weights, and in this *Wine Measures* are specifically mentioned, as follows:

Gallon 10 lbs. each
pottle 6 lbs. each
quart 3 lbs. each
pint 2 lbs. each
$\frac{1}{2}$-pint 1 lb. each
$\frac{1}{4}$-pint 8 lbs. per dozen
half $\frac{1}{4}$-pint, 4 lbs. the dozen

Note that the smallest listed size is the 'half $\frac{1}{4}$-pint', or, in other words, the half-gill. There is no mention here, or later in the Company records, of the very small measure, the $\frac{1}{4}$-gill, specimens of which have turned up, from time to time, and have been accepted by some collectors as genuine. In the writer's opinion, *all* of the $\frac{1}{4}$-gill measures which have come to his notice are faked pieces.

The above list of sizes includes the full range of baluster-shaped Wine Measures which we know today, and there is little doubt that the list does, in fact, refer to that type of measure.

At this period the baluster measure was being made with a thumbpiece resembling a hammer, and it is known universally among collectors as the 'hammerhead' type. (See Fig. 36.)

Still earlier types of thumbpieces were either of 'wedge' formation, or of a wedge upon which a ball was perched, and the latter were known as 'ball and wedge'. Figs. 34 and 35 show excellent examples of these types.

Although baluster measures are known to collectors by the terms indicative of their capacities (as in the given list), the capacity is that relative to the Old English Wine Standard, and not to Imperial measure as used for most liquids today. The Old Wine Standard was five-sixths of Imperial measure, the comparative table being as follows:

O.E.W.S.			Imperial Standard
Gallon .	. 133·3		160
½-gallon.	. 66·6		80
quart	. 33·3	fluid	40
pint	. 16·6	ounces	20
½-pint .	. 8·3		10
gill	. 4·15		5
½-gill .	. 2·07		2·5

It is interesting to note that the United States liquid standard still conforms to the Old English Wine Standard, i.e. 16·6 fluid ozs to the pint.

There are five main types of English lidded baluster measures, and several types of similar measures without covers. Of the lidded types the first three have already been mentioned.

Measures of 'hammerhead' type were superseded by those with 'Bud and wedge' thumbpiece (shown in Fig. 37).

This was followed by a type known as 'Double Volute', and it is this type which is most frequently found today. (See Fig. 38.)

Accurate dating of the commencement and longevity of each group is difficult owing to the fact that provincial pewterers frequently lagged behind those of London and other busy pewtering centres but, allowing for some overlapping during the transitional stages, it may be said that the 'ball and wedge' was in use up to c.1650, probably coeval with the 'wedge', and that the 'hammerhead' came into popularity about this time. We are able to date the latter with more accuracy owing to the numbers of marked specimens which have come down to us, and it can be said that the type was unlikely to have been made in any quantity (if at all) after c.1700.

Measures with 'bud' thumbpiece were made by London pewterers as early as 1680, and the type persisted well into the 18th century to c.1740, or even later in the case of the larger sizes.

The 'double volute' thumbpiece seems to have come into prominence during the second quarter of the 18th century, and held the field throughout the remaining years and on into the early 19th century.

It is one of the greatest mysteries why one style of thumb-piece was dropped comparatively abruptly, and was super-seded by another several times throughout the usage of a similar body style.

Nothing in the Pewterers' Company records, as published, gives us any clue to the reason, but it would almost seem that edicts went out from time to time to enforce that henceforth all baluster measures must be made with a thumbpiece con-forming to a given pattern. No matter where the measures were made, the variations in any particular type are negligible, despite the fact that they might have been made in different and widely separated parts of the country, and at widely divergent dates.

Scottish pewterers adopted the baluster style of body, and it is possible that some of the aforementioned types may have been made in Scotland, although none of the earlier types have been found with Scottish makers' marks. The thumb-pieces which can be definitely linked with Scotland are, firstly, the 'ball and bar'; this is distinguished from the earlier English 'ball and wedge' principally by the shape of the bar of metal upon the cover, and upon which the ball is perched. A glance at the fine English measure in Fig. 35 will show the distinct sloping wedge, whereas that in Fig. 39 shows a typical Scottish 'ball' thumbpiece. In the latter type the lid appendage is almost straight, but does sometimes slope to a lesser extent than the English.

The more familiar Scottish thumbpiece—the 'embryo-shell'—is so named because of its supposed resemblance to a cockle shell which has not yet acquired the ridges apparent on most sea shells of the type. There is a well-known varia-tion which has missed the notice of most previous writers, and to which the present writer has given the title 'Spade' thumbpiece. (See drawing.)

FIG. 5. Thumbpiece on Scottish baluster measures, likened to a gravedigger's spade. (Early 19th century.)

Collectors should have no difficulty in deciding the provenance of Scottish measures, for beneath the lids of the latter there is always a raised flange of metal which prevents the lid, when closed, from sliding from side to side and thus weakening the hinge.

The 'ball and bar' type came into general use towards the end of the 18th century, although very occasionally one finds a measure with this style of appendage which is undoubtedly very much earlier, but until marked specimens appear their earliest date must remain conjectural. These were closely followed by the 'embryo-shell' and 'spade' variations, which can be dated from *c.*1800 or thereabouts. These latter types continued in popularity until at least 1860.

Having dealt with Scottish baluster measures, it may be as well to run briefly through the other styles of measures produced in that country.

The earliest of all known Scottish measures were what are commonly known as 'pot-bellied' measures, and are found both lidded and unlidded. The type is peculiar to Scotland, and the style was undoubtedly borrowed from the Continent. 'Pot-belly' measures are rare, and date from *c.*1680 to, perhaps, 1740.

The popular term 'Tappit Hen' is the familiar title bestowed on the essentially Scottish type of wine measure shown in Fig. 41.

Measures of this type are found in a long range of sizes, including both Imperial and Scottish standard capacity. The term 'tappit hen' is said to have been derived from the word 'Topynet', a French measure of *capacity*, and was soon corrupted by the Scots into the word 'tappit hen' which has persisted (and, doubtless, will continue to do so) for at least two centuries.

The true 'tappit hen' is a measure of one Scots pint capacity; a Scots pint being equivalent to three English (or Imperial) pints.

Originally these measures were made in three sizes only, viz., the tappit hen, already described; the 'Chopin', which contains 1½ Imperial pints; and the 'Mutchkin', equivalent to ¾ of an Imperial pint.

As the English standard came to be adopted in the early 19th century other sizes were made in the same form. The earliest dated tappit hen is noted by Ingleby Wood as bearing a touch dated 1669, and this must be looked upon as being the grandmother of all tappit hens, even if we allow that its maker may have had a working life of some forty years. This particular specimen is of 'chopin' capacity, and is housed in the Museum of Antiquities at Edinburgh.

Most of the measures of tappit hen form which one comes across today date from about the mid-18th century to the early or mid-19th century.

'Crested' tappit hens are later in the field than those with domed cover, and were made in the three Scots sizes only. It is doubtful if any with knopped cover were made prior to 1780. They had a comparatively short life, and are not easily come by today.

By far the most common of Scottish measures are those with a pear-shaped body and domed cover. These are usually of early 19th-century period, but, occasionally, specimens dating up to c.1860 are found. At about this date was sounded the death knell for pewter, as a general commodity, and from

this time onwards little seems to have been made but ugly
tavern pots of small interest to collectors.

During the first quarter of the 19th century a type of

FIG. 6. Scottish thistle-shaped measure,
c.1830. These measures have been found
in a range of sizes, from the 1-pint (Imperial) to the small Scots measure ⅛-gill.

measure shaped like a thistle was evolved in Scotland, but it
had a short life, and genuine specimens are rare.

By an Act of 1907 it was made necessary for all measures to
empty when tilted to an angle of 120 degrees. Thistle measures
could not do this and, thus, were regarded as 'facilitating the
perpetration of fraud'. In the majority of cases, when they

FIG. 7. Irish 'Haystack', or 'Harvester'
measure. (Early 19th century.) These
measures are found in a range of eight sizes,
from the gallon (Imperial) to the ¼-gill.

were submitted to Inspectors for verification of their capacities,
they were destroyed, which, no doubt, accounts for their
present rarity.

Irish pewterers seem to have remained aloof from the influence of both England and Scotland, and the types of measures best known to collectors as originating there are 'Haystack' (or 'Harvester') measures, and small handleless baluster measures, known locally as 'Noggins'. Neither type seems to have been made prior to the 19th century, and it is

FIG. 8. A set of four Irish lidless baluster-shaped measures, from the ½-pint to the ¼-gill (Imperial). (Early 19th century.)

probable that measures in earlier use were imported from England.

Before bringing to a close this chapter on measures one must not overlook the essentially English Spirit Measures, known as 'Bristol', or 'West Country' measures. It is probable that the term originated from the fact that Bristol has been, (and still is) one of the main centres of export for distilled spirits, and it is a fact that this type of measure is not found in other parts of the country.

Be that as it may, the name has become the recognized term to designate the type. (See Fig. 9.)

Specimens dating from the mid-18th century have been

found, and whilst some show definite variations in contour the same general features are constant. It is doubtful if they were made in pewter later than *c.*1830, although copper measures of the same general type were made and used, at least, up to the early 20th century.

The Channel Islands have produced a type of measure, quite different from anything made elsewhere in the British

FIG. 9. 'Bristol', or 'West Country', bulbous spirit measure. (Early 19th century.) These measures (some varying very slightly in contour) are found from the gallon to the ½-gill.

Isles. There is, possibly quite naturally, a Continental influence to be seen in these pieces, and a glance at the illustrations will confirm this statement. The twin-acorn thumbpiece, for example, is not found on any other type of British pewter, but it does turn up on several French and Flemish measures and flagons. In fact, the adoption of this thumbpiece is the direct result of the former use of French measures in the Islands in the early to mid-18th century.

Few, if any, of the Channel Islands types can be dated earlier than about 1750 or so.

The Guernsey measures in Fig. 43 are of elongated pearshape, with a heart-shaped hinged cover. These differ from the Jersey type in that the former have a moulded foot rim and, usually, have bands of reeding round the neck and belly. Guernsey measures were made in three sizes only.

Those from Jersey are much plainer in style, and are made in a fuller range of sizes; and are also found in lidless forms.

The illustration, Fig. 44, shows a full range of Jersey lidded measures; the lidless Jersey type extends to only five, the largest size being omitted.

BIBLIOGRAPHY

CLAPPERTON, LEWIS: 'Some Scottish Pewter Measures', *Antiques* (U.S.A.), February, 1948.

COTTERELL, H. H.: 'The Tappit Hen', *Bazaar, Exchange and Mart*, 27th April, 1923.

—— 'Pewter Baluster Measures', *Connoisseur*, August, 1919.

—— 'Scottish Pewter Measures', *Connoisseur*, May, 1931.

—— 'Old Pewter Wine Vessels', *Wine Trade Review*, 20th March, 27th March, 10th April, 1931.

—— 'Early Pewter Baluster Measures' (an explanation of their lid markings), *Apollo*, May, 1933.

MAY, H. E.: 'Old Pewter' (Scottish Measures), *Country Life*, 18th September, 1915.

MICHAELIS, RONALD F.: 'Old Pewter Wine Measures', in *Antique Collector*, Part I, February, 1953; Part II, August, 1953.

—— 'Capacity Marks on Old English Pewter Measures', *Antique Collector*, August, 1954.

——'Early Stuart Pewter at Cotehele, Cornwall', *Antique Collector*, February, 1959.

——'Capacities of Scottish Measures (Tappit Hen Shaped)', in *Libra, Journal of the Weights & Measures Administration*, September and December, 1965. (Reprinted in the *Bulletin of the Pewter Collectors' Club of America*.)

MYRTLE, J. H.: '18th Century Baluster Measures', *Antique Collector*, February, 1954.

PEAL, CHRISTOPHER: 'Tankards, and "Housemarks" on Early Measures', *Apollo*, June, 1949.

—— 'Notes on Pewter Baluster Measures, and their Capacities', *Apollo*, January, 1950.

SHELLEY, ROLAND J. A.: 'A Stuart Pewter Measure', *Apollo*, October, 1946.

SPEIGHT, HAROLD W.: 'Verification Marks on Old Pewter Measures', *Antique Collector*, December, 1938.

SUTHERLAND GRAEME, A. V.: 'Pewter of the Channel Islands', *Antique Collector*, May, 1938.

CHAPTER FIVE

CANDLESTICKS, SALTS AND SPOONS

As WITH other articles made in pewter, the records of candlesticks and candlestick making go back to a much earlier period than do the specimens which have survived.

Inventories and wills of the 14th century make frequent mention of candlesticks, and there is no doubt that pewter candlesticks were in use, both in the home and in the churches and abbeys, at least from the 13th century.

The earliest records known to the writer are in the lists of official Visitations of Devonshire Churches between the years 1301 and 1330 where, for example, we find: (at Dawlish, 5th July, 1301) 'Two very beautiful processional candlesticks, and four of pewter'; and (at Colyton, on 10th July, 1301) 'Two small candlesticks of pewter for procession'.[1]

The first mention of candlesticks in the records of the Pewterers' Company is in 1562–3, and it is not until 1612–3 that any specific details are given by which extant types might be recognized. In that year a quantity of 'tryffles' were assayed by the Company, and a standard of weights for each type was set up. The list is quoted as given in the records, and explanations' of terms will be given where possible.

Ould fashion Candlesticks	Ordinarie highe c'sticks, to weigh, per pair 3¼ lbs.
	Greate middle, to weigh, per pair 2 lbs. 2 oz.
	Greate pyller, to weigh, per pair 3 lbs.
	Smale middel, to weigh, per pair 2¼ lbs.
	Middle pyller, to weigh, per pair 2½ lbs.
Geo. Smythe	⎰ Smale fashion, to weigh, per pair 2½ lbs.
	⎱ Greate New fashion, to weigh, per pair 3 lbs.

---

[1] *Visitations of Devonshire Churches*, by H. Michael Whitley, in Trans. of Devonshire Assn., Vol. XLII, July, 1910.

Greate bell, to weigh, per pair 3½ lbs.
low bell, to weigh, per pair 2 lbs.
Greate Wryteinge, to weigh, per pair 1½ lbs.
Midd. Wryteinge, to weigh, per pair 1 lb.
Smale Wryteinge, to weigh, per pair ¾ lb.

Candlesticks Grawnd, to weigh, per pair 4½ lbs.
  with   Ordinarie highe, to weigh, per pair 3¼ lbs.
  bawles   Greate Middle, to weigh, per pair 2 lbs. 2 oz.
          Small middle, to weigh, per pair 2¼ lbs.
          Great Wryteinge, to weigh, per pair 1½ lbs.

George Smythe's name is given in the margin, and it is supposed that the styles closely associated with his name were his particular specialities.

'Candlesticks with bawles' are, doubtless, candlesticks with ball knopped columns.

Only two of these descriptions, i.e. 'Greate bell' and 'low bell', seem to fit any of the early specimens which are known today, and if this is so they would apply to the fine bell-based candlesticks shown in Figs. 45 and 46.

We still have much to learn of the early forms, and whilst it is believed that, of those we know, most are of the mid-17th century and later, it is possible that some may relate to 1612 or thereabouts.

The 'Grainger' candlestick in the Victoria and Albert Museum is the earliest *dated* example we have. This is almost too well-known to need further illustration, but readers may be interested to know that as part of its cast decoration it bears a representation of the Arms of the Pewterers' Company and also the Rose and Crown in addition to the name and date 'William Granger, 1616'.

William Grainger was made a Freeman pewterer of London in 1597; was Searcher for the Company in 1612; Steward in 1620; Renter Warden in 1628, and Upper Warden in 1638.

The illustrations at Figs. 47 and 48 show a variety of 17th-century candlesticks, all of which are essentially English, and of which very similar contemporary examples may be found in silver.

The octagonal base was a popular feature up to, at least, the beginning of the reign of Queen Anne, and is occasionally found in Georgian examples. At this time, however, the central drip-tray tends to disappear, and the candlesticks assume a purely baluster effect.

Pewter candlesticks of the mid to late 18th century are rarely met with, and it is thought that brass and silver 'sticks were found to be of more lasting use. One reason which makes pewter less suitable for this class of object is its liability to melt when the candle burns low and concentrates too much heat on the top flange.

This would have been no less the case in the earlier specimens, but be that as it may, there are certainly more 17th-century pewter candlesticks in collections today than there are of mid to late 18th-century types.

At the turn of the 18th century pewter candlesticks again came into their own, and many pleasing tall baluster types are found. These follow the general styles adopted by the braziers, and usually have an ingenious push-rod inserted in the column; its function being to eject small sections of candle which remain below the sconce flange. Such candlesticks were made up to about the middle of the reign of Queen Victoria.

There is often to be found an affinity between the base castings of some 17th-century candlesticks and those of contemporary salts.

In fact, it is probable that the identical moulds were used for both.

The earliest types of Salts, of which, unfortunately, no examples are known to exist, were many and varied. In 1438 we read of 'plaine Salers'; 'Cowped Salers'; 'plaine small salers', and 'short Salers', and in 1550 an Inventory of goods of the Pewterers' Company includes 'vj Salte Syllers, w'out covers' and 'vj Salte sellers with cover that was had of Mr.

Blackwall'. Shortly after this—in 1551-2—the Pewterers' Court considered the punishment of certain pewterers for making 'certayne Salts which were made of laye mettall—which ought to have been made of fyne mettall', and decreed that from henceforth 'no man shall make salts other than iiij s. salts and iij s. salts and Chopnets Grate and small after the olde fashion . . .', and that 'no man shall make salts of any new fashion without it be allowed and adjudged by the Master & Wardens except it be of fine metal'.

It is, perhaps, of interest to note that the term Salt-Celler is actually an English corruption. The French word 'saliere', meaning Salt Holder, becoming corrupted to cellar, or saler, and thus, when used together with the word salt, is superfluous.

In ancient times salt was one of the most precious of culinary essentials, so much so that it was customary, in early Roman times, for all or part of the wages paid to servants and soldiers to be made in the form of salt. In later days this came to be replaced by money or other gifts in kind, but the term 'salary' persists to this day.

Salt became the medium by which rank and precedence was defined at table. It was customary for the head of the household, or Master, and his most prominent guests, to be seated at a table set upon a dais; this being known as the high table. The other tables were placed on the floor level abutting the high table. Even today this arrangement is followed at banquets and similar functions, although the elevated table has now disappeared.

The salt would be placed to the front and slightly to the right of the Master, and the distance of each guest from the salt indicated his social status. Thus—as today—the principal guest was placed on the right hand of the Master, and so he was as near to the salt as his host, and the rest of the assembly were placed to the left or right in order of precedence.

Salt was placed at a certain point down the length of the

supplementary table and, here again, the more important guests were placed 'above the salt'.

Salt, therefore, being of such importance it is not surprising to find that excellent workmanship was put into some of the earliest known examples.

As with candlesticks, there are considerable numbers of late 17th-century salts in existence, and, because of their pleasing designs, they are ever popular with collectors.

Types range from the large Master Salts to the smaller Capstans, which latter were made in a variety of styles during the last quarter of the 17th century. Salts of about the year 1700 were made in a more globular form, and this type gave way, in turn, to footed types with larger bowls, known as 'Cup Salts'.

The earliest salts will be found to have mere depressions in the top to hold only small quantities of salt but, gradually, as salt became more easily procurable, the bowls became larger and deeper.

In the later cup-salts there is to be found infinite variety of style, and specimens dating up to about 1780 or so are well worthy of acquisition by serious collectors. Even later examples can be used with excellent effect as ashtrays or sugar bowls, and will not disgrace any table.

Excluding Roman pewter, the earliest objects in pewter which have frequently been dug up from excavations in London and elsewhere, are Spoons—some dating from as early as the 14th century.

They have survived probably because of their smallness and comparative solidity, and they form, by themselves, an exceptionally interesting class of collectable objects, needing very little space for display.

To quote the late F. G. Hilton Price, whose book on the study of base metal spoons is still looked upon as the standard work on the subject, it can be said that 'nearly all English examples, whether made of base metal or silver, from the

14th century to the middle of the 17th century, had fig-shaped bowls curving upwards, being broader at the base and narrower near the stalk or stem. The stems were "six-squared" or hexagonal, and terminated in most cases with a knop, which varied according to existing fashion or the vagary of the spoonmaker'. Thus, it is the knops themselves which, by their very variety, make such an interesting study.

In most cases these were copied by the pewterers from known and datable examples in silver, but there are some rare types in pewter which are not known in silver and *vice versa.*

The earliest English pewter spoons are probably those with a 'ball' knop and rather longer stem than usual. Hilton Price dated such examples as of the late 14th or early 15th century.

Other early knops were made in the shape of 'cones', and some with what looked like small 'crowns', which latter have become known as 'Finial' knops.

It is not unusual to find pewter spoons with brass or 'latten' knops. In fact, both 'Cone' and 'Finial' types were frequently made in that way, and are easily datable for that very reason

The records of the Pewterers' Company make mention, in 1562–3, of 'spoons with latten knops', and in 1567–8, and in 1586–7, makers of pewter spoons were evidently also making them wholly of latten, although this was expressly forbidden by the Company.

The last time latten knops are mentioned being in 1619–20, when one Robert Austin was fined 'for burneing latten knopped spoones with course mettal'. This referred to the attachment of knops with a solder of inferior metal to that from which the spoon itself was made. It is doubtful if latten knops were made after *c.*1625.

Another popular form of knop was the 'Acorn'; an inventory of plate belonging to the Cathedral Church of Lincoln, taken in 1548, mentions 'a spoone with an Akerne, ordeined for Creame', and 'a spoone with an Akerne, ordeined for Oleum'.

These examples were, doubtless, earlier than the date of the inventory.

Spoons with 'Akerne' knops are mentioned in 1348 and 1351, but these were of silver; nevertheless it is probable that pewter examples were made within a very short time of the first appearance of silver specimens.

Spoons with 'diamond pointed' knops are very rare in pewter, and can be dated as of the 15th century.

Another rare spoon of this early period is that with 'Horned Head-dress' knop. The knop represents the bust of a woman wearing the peculiar horned, or horseshoe, form of headwear which was fashionable in the reigns of Henry V and Henry VI. It is unlikely that they were made later than the end of the 15th century.

There are other forms of knops representing female busts, and these are usually known as 'Maidenhead' knops, probably depicting the Blessed Virgin.   These, and others with 'Monk's Head' and 'Alderman' knops, probably date from the mid-15th century to early in the 17th century.

Rare types indeed are 'Lion Sejant' (the sitting lion), and 'Chanticlier' (the Cock), both of the late 16th century.

We find that the commoner silver types, such as 'Sealtops', 'Baluster knops' and 'Strawberry knops' are all represented in pewter, and so, too, the 'Apostle'. Whereas, in silver—if one's pocket is deep enough—it is possible to complete a set of thirteen items, including the Master, or 'Christ' knop, it would prove a fruitless task for any pewter enthusiast to attempt the feat.   Apostles were made both in pewter and latten from the mid-15th century to well into the 17th century, but only a few of the twelve Apostles have come to light.

Probably the commonest of all English pewter spoons are those known as 'Slip top', or 'Slipped in the Stalk'.   Spoons of this type have the usual fig-shaped bowls and hexagonal or sexagonal stems, with the end cut off slantwise from the front of the spoon.

The earlier forms were somewhat slender in the stem, but towards the end of the 16th century and the beginning of the 17th century they were made generally stouter and stronger, the base of the stems having a short tongue which extended into, and helped to support the weight of, the bowl. This type, in one or another of its various forms, remained in fashion until the mid-17th century, when it was succeeded by a type with flattened stem known as the 'Puritan'. At about this time there was a radical change in the shape of spoon bowls.

With the 'Puritan' the bowl was made in a true egg-shaped outline, broader at the top than at the lower end, still however very shallow.

The last of the 17th-century types was undoubtedly evolved from the Puritan, and seems to have been produced by hammering the top of the stem into a broader, and almost circular flat disc.

This was cut obliquely with two deep notches—one at either side—which widened into definite 'V's as the hammering continued, and gave the effect of a crude three-leaf clover. The type became known as 'Split end', 'Trifid' or 'Pied de Biche'; the latter term derived from France and applied because the shape was supposed to bear some resemblance to the cloven hoof of a deer.

There are endless variations in the shapes of this beaten 'split-end', and it is seldom that one finds two exactly alike.

It is only towards the end of the life of this type that shaped moulds, which actually cast the top in the 'trifid' shape, were used to make the more elaborate forms. Some of these bear cast embossed decoration, obviously slavishly copied from Continental examples which had gained favour with the return of Charles II in 1660.

Spoons with cast portraits of Royalty as part of the terminal decoration were made in the late 17th century; the first recognizable portraits being of William III and Mary. Later William, alone, is depicted and, in due course, Queen Anne.

There is an endless variety of such cast decorated Royal portrait spoons which make an interesting special study.

With the advent of the Georges we have spoons with longer stems and more slender bowls, known to collectors of silver and pewter spoons alike as 'Hanoverian' pattern. Chief among these is a revival of the cast Royal portrait type, made to commemorate the marriage of George III and his Consort, Charlotte Sophia, of Mecklenburg Strelitz, in 1761.

This, and other Royal portrait commemorative specimens, are to be seen in the hanging rack in Fig. 51.

Some earlier types, also attractively displayed in an old oak Spoonrack, are shown in Fig. 52.

BIBLIOGRAPHY

COTTERELL, H. H.: 'Some Early Pewter Candlesticks', *Connoisseur*, February, 1934.
—— 'Four Pewter Altar Candlesticks in York Minster', *Burlington Magazine*, May, 1931.
GASK, NORMAN: 'Mediaeval Pewter Spoons', *Apollo*, December, 1949.
HODGSON, MRS. WILLOUGHBY: 'The English Silver Spoon', *Apollo*, October, 1943.
HUGHES, G. BERNARD: 'Old Pewter Spoons', *Country Life*, 26th November, 1953.
MICHAELIS, RONALD F.: 'Royal Portrait Spoons in Pewter', *Apollo*, June, 1950.
PEAL, CHRISTOPHER A.: 'Pewter Salts, Candlesticks and Some Plates', *Apollo*, May, 1949.
——'English Knopped Latten Spoons', in two parts, *Connoisseur*, April and July, 1970.
PORT, CHARLES G. J.: 'Some Continental Base Metal Spoons', *Connoisseur*, December, 1912.
SUTHERLAND GRAEME, A. V.: 'Types of Old Pewter Spoons', *Bazaar, Exchange and Mart*, 27th October, 1936.
—— 'Pewter Spoons', *Connoisseur*, December, 1947.
WENHAM, EDWARD: 'Salt Cellars', *Antique Collector*, April, 1948.

CHAPTER SIX

PORRINGERS, BLEEDING BOWLS, CAUDLE CUPS, ETC.

EAR DISHES, or Porringers, are first mentioned in the London records in 1556-7 (13th March) where it is ordained that 'no person (of the Company) shall from henceforth make, or cause to be made, any eare disshes fflower delice (fleur de lis) or any other manner of eares except suche eares be cast in the mowlde together with the body of suche disshes so made and not to bc sothered (soldered) to the body as heretofore they have done'. In this case we can trace the actual type of vessel indicated, for the Guildhall and London museums can both show specimens of mid-16th century two-eared porringers *cast in one piece, and bearing ears in the form of fleurs des lis.*

Fig. 10(a) illustrates a specimen of these Elizabethan ear dishes from the Guildhall Museum. There is, however, a type of porringer of somewhat similar style, but of cruder workman-ship and design, an example of which is shown in Fig. 10(b). Several specimens of this type are extant in London museums and elsewhere, and they are believed to be of even earlier date than that first mentioned.

From about the beginning of the 17th century it was more common for porringers to be made with one ear only and, almost without exception, this rule holds during the whole period of their manufacture.

During the first half of the 17th century the bowl of English porringers was with a flat base, sometimes bossed in the centre, and with straight sides sloping outwards towards the top. The more familiar 'booged' bowl, i.e. with curved and bulging sides and small collar to the brim, came into use about 1650 or so, and the shape persisted until *c.*1750, after which the

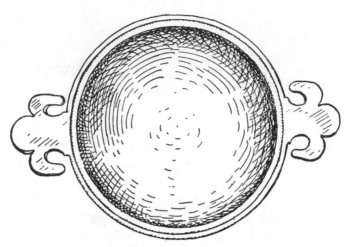

FIG. 10A. An Elizabethan or James I period, two-eared porringer, with 'fleur de lys' ears. (From the Guildhall Museum, London.)

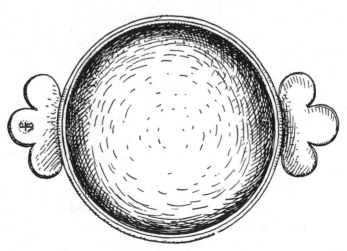

FIG. 10B. An Elizabethan porringer, of cruder design, but of which several specimens are known in public and private collections.

manufacture of pewter porringers practically ceased; their place evidently being taken by pottery and porcelain vessels.

The illustrations show typical specimens of English single-eared porringers from c.1625–1750. (See Figs. 53, 54, 55.)

Blood porringers, or bleeding bowls as they are sometimes called, are first mentioned in 1659–60, but so far as is known, at this time they bore no distinguishing features to separate them from normal porringers.

In the records for 1673–4, where the list of weights for specific types of vessels is quoted, 'Bossed porringers', of six sizes, varying in weight from 7 lbs to 2 lbs per dozen, are given.

'Ordinary blood porringers' are stated to weigh 1½ lbs per dozen.

The weight of 2 ozs for each piece would indicate a vessel of approximately 3 inches diameter. Such small items would normally be classed as wine tasters as, for example, the tiny specimen with decorated centre boss in Fig. 87.

A more modern type of bleeding bowl is shown in Fig. 56; the illustration clearly shows the gradation marks inside the bowl, measured off in 2 oz levels. In this example there is a revival of the early 'straight-sided' porringer bowl, and this style, usually with the more conventional pierced ear, was used frequently in hospitals for various purposes in the late 18th and early 19th centuries.

'Cawdle Pots', or Caudle cups, are first mentioned in 1612–3, and were, doubtless, cups with two handles, of the same general style of that shown in Figs. 24 and 57. Many types of two-handled cups were produced in the 17th and 18th centuries, and the style continued into the early years of the 19th century.

Various titles have been given to these cups, such as Caudle cups; Posset pots; Wassail bowls; Toasting cups and Loving cups, and it may be as well to decide into which category they shall be placed.

The primary factors for consideration are the number of handles on the pieces in question, and the overall sizes of the pots in relation to each other.

A cup of deeper bowl than the normal porringer, with either one or two handles, would come within the category of Caudle or Posset cup.

A Caudle was a drink consisting of wines, spices and other ingredients and, in its earlier form, was in the nature of a thin gruel.

It was generally of a semi-medicinal nature and was given to sick persons, especially to women at childbirth.

Posset was generally made with cream, sugar and nutmeg, curdled with ale or sack, and thickened with small pieces of bread. Thus, it is probable that the latter, being thicker and having to be eaten with a spoon, would require a wider-mouthed receptacle than caudle.

However, this is purely conjectural, and it is not possible in these pages to lay down any hard and fast rule.

One fact worthy of mention is that a similarly shaped vessel in silver is invariably called a porringer, whereas the latter term is reserved by pewter collectors to cover only the shallow vessels dealt with in the first part of this chapter.

Wassail bowls and toasting cups would necessarily be of much larger proportions, since the whole essence of the Wassail was an occasion of festivity at which healths were drunk, and it is obvious that a wassail bowl should be able to contain sufficient liquor to pass from mouth to mouth, *and* that it should have handles for safe holding in the process.

When used for drinking a parting toast it was usual for the one who had just drunk to retain hold of one handle until his neighbour had taken his sip whilst grasping the other, and so the bowl passed round the assembly—the handles linking the members in friendship as it went. Fig. 58 illustrates a typical wassail bowl.

From this type of bowl originated the Loving cups, but the

latter are, generally, more personal vessels, probably presented as keepsakes to married couples on their wedding day or anniversary.

This would account for their smaller sizes, and the frequency of dated or initialled specimens.   A three-handled cup would almost certainly be a loving cup.

FIG. 11.   A group of late 18th- and early 19th-century loving cups.

There are very few, if any, footed loving cups which can be dated earlier than, say, 1750.   All those illustrated in Fig. 11 are late, and belong to either the end of the 18th century, or, perhaps, to the first quarter of the 19th century.

These have been classed as loving cups simply because they display two handles, but it is quite possible that some were merely domestic drinking cups, or possibly even vases or ornaments.

The plain footed cups and single-handled examples in the next illustration are, doubtless, purely domestic cups for

FIG. 12. A selection of early
19th-century domestic footed cups.

everyday use, and are all of early 19th-century date. (See Fig. 12.)

BIBLIOGRAPHY

COTTERELL, HOWARD H.: 'Porringers, Caudle, Posset and Toasting Cups', in *Apollo*, Part I, August, 1938; Part II, March, 1939; Part III, October, 1942.

MICHAELIS, RONALD F.: 'English Pewter Porringers', in *Apollo*, Part I, July, 1949; Part II, August, 1949; Part III, September, 1949; Part IV, October, 1949.

——'English Commemorative Porringers in Pewter', *Antique Collector*, October, 1956.

——'Royal Portraits and Pewter Porringers', *Antiques*, January, 1958.

——'More about English Commemorative Porringers', *Antiques*, July, 1960.

——'Creation Porringer in Pewter', *Antiques*, June, 1964.

——'Royal Occasions Commemorated in English Pewter', *Antique Collector*, August and September, 1966.

CHAPTER SEVEN

ECCLESIASTICAL PEWTER
Flagons, Chalices, Patens, Alms Dishes, Etc.

WHEN ONE CONTEMPLATES the beautiful silver altar vessels which grace so many of our churches today, it is difficult to realize that there have been periods in the past when the church was accustomed to use vessels of pewter for its highest services.

The first official recognition of pewter as a substance suitable for a chalice, is to be traced to the Synod which assembled at Rouen in the year 1074, at which the use of wood for that purpose was forbidden, and the adoption of pewter allowed, in cases where it was found impossible to provide vessels of rarer metal. A similar resolution was passed by the Council of Winchester some two years later.

At a Council held at Westminster, however, a century later, the further use of pewter for this purpose was proscribed, and it was decreed that, for the future, only vessels of gold or silver should be consecrated. This limitation was intended to apply only to such vessels as were to be used actually in the services of the church.

In *The Church Plate of Wiltshire*,[1] the author reminds us that by the constitutions of William de Blois, Bishop of Worcester, A.D. 1229, two Chalices were to be required for every church, one of silver for use at Mass, and the other to be unconsecrated and fashioned of *tin*, to be placed in the coffin of the priest at his burial.

Sepulchral chalices and patens have been found, from time to time, in the coffins and graves of Church dignitaries, and specimens have been illustrated in several publications written for collectors.

[1] Rev. J. E. Nightingale, 1891 edition, p. 5.

For example, a fine specimen of wide-mouthed tazza-shaped chalice with its attendant paten, found in a tomb which can be dated as early as 1269, is illustrated by de Navarro,[1] and also by Cotterell[2], together with another of very similar form, from the grave of a priest at Witham on the Hill, Lincs.

An almost identical pair, comprising a wide-mouthed chalice and a shallow paten, were found in 1913, in a stone coffin in the east aisle of the north transept of Westminster Abbey. The grave is almost certainly that of Abbot Richard de Berkyng, who died in 1246.

Several other examples of 13th- and 14th-century pewter chalices can be called to mind and, in all cases, they are of the same form.

It is, naturally, mainly from church records that we can derive any information of the types of articles used for sacred purposes, and one fact, in particular, stands out as being in need of an explanation. Frequent 15th- and 16th-century references can be found relating to pewter cruets, i.e. the small covered vessels used to contain the wine and water necessary for altar purposes, but we have, as yet, no first-hand knowledge of their style or shape—we must assume, however, that they followed the pattern of contemporary silver examples; several specimens of which exist today.

There is no doubt that, in the wealthier churches, cruets (and other vessels) of silver would have been in use, but with the spoliation of the churches by Edward IV, when it became evident that the parish churches were to be stripped of their superfluous plate, it was most likely that these cruets were among the first items to go.

During the reign of Mary I, however, a temporary reaction came about, and such cruets as had been sold, but which were, nevertheless, required by the injunctions of Bishop Bonner

---

[1] *Causeries on English Pewter*, London & New York, 1911, p. 160.
[2] *Old Pewter*, London, 1929. Plate XXVIII (a) and (d).

(1554) to be found in every church, would probably have been replaced by vessels of pewter.

In fact, the church accounts of Waltham Holy Cross, for example, specifically state that, at this date, certain vessels of pewter were obtained to replace those which had been sold or made away with during the previous reign. That these pewter cruets, which must at this time have formed part of the communion vessels in most churches, have not survived may be explained by the fact that since their provision would have been made under Papist influence, they would, in the reign of Elizabeth I, have been looked upon by the more extreme reformers as coming within the category of 'feigned monuments of superstition' and treated accordingly.

Of the comparatively few pewter cruets which have come to light up to the present day it is safe to say that only one or two might be able to claim English, or even British, nationality. It is rare to find a maker's mark which bears any resemblance to those on early English pewter, and the inference must be that the majority, if not all, are foreign.

It is a fact that there is more early church pewter in existence today than there is of contemporary pewter used solely for domestic purposes. This is not surprising, bearing in mind that many of the ecclesiastical vessels will have been consecrated for use in the church, and, in many cases, even after their usefulness had been spent, they would have been preserved by the Church Wardens, or custodians, as relics worthy of retention. It is probable that, at least until the middle of the 19th century, most of the flagons which now grace private collections were still in the keeping of the churches for which they were made, and that these have been alienated only since the collecting of antique pewter became more general.

This trend had something of a fillip in the early years of the 20th century, when several books on pewter and pewter collecting were brought out, in addition to the publication of the History of the Pewterers' Company, to which reference

has so frequently been made in this book. The Exhibitions
of Pewter, staged at Clifford's Inn Hall, in 1904 and 1908, by
the late H. J. L. J. Massé, were also instrumental in adding
numerous collectors to the ranks.

With the greater demand for fine and early specimens it is
small wonder that prices began to rise and, in consequence,
many churches which owned pewter vessels of one sort or
another, but which had no further use for them owing to
their replacement by more elaborate silver or silver-plated
pieces, parted with them gladly in exchange for a few pounds
towards the upkeep of the church, or for funds to augment
some other (let us hope) equally worthy cause.

It is, of course, evident that many scores of pewter communion flagons of all dates still remain in the parish churches
to which they belong; many more have been 'alienated',
undoubtedly without any legal permission. It cannot be
too strongly emphasised that church vessels are held in trust,
and that alienation of them without a Faculty is illegal, but
the fact remains that, either by ignorance or design, many
more flagons have left their original homes than there have
been faculties granted.

It can be said, however, that by whatever cause they came
upon the market they have now found a more appreciative
home than was the case with the majority during their final
ownership by the church.

Although flagons were in use for communicants in the reign
of Edward VI, when, in 1547, the laity were readmitted to
Holy Communion, no pewter flagons of the period are known
to exist; and only one is known which can, conceivably, belong
to the reign of Elizabeth I.

This flagon is illustrated at Fig. 60, and, although several
silver flagons of comparable shape are in existence, no others
in pewter—either of this pleasing pear-shape, or of any other
style, belonging to the first Elizabethan period—have so far
been recognised.

The promulgation of the Canons of 1603—the 20th being an injunction that the sacramental wine should be 'brought to the communion table in a clean and sweet standing pot or stoup of pewter, if not of purer metal', led to a considerable increase in the numbers of pewter flagons in the churches from that date onwards.

These early flagons are of tapering cylindrical form, upon a moulded foot, with plain single-curved handle, and a 'bun' or 'muffin-shaped' cover. (Figs. 61 and 62.) Towards the middle of the 17th century the foot was made much wider than formerly, and this tended to make the flagon much more steady. (See Fig. 63.)

The cover used with this 'spread' base type has been likened to the cap worn by the Yeomen of the Guard at the Tower of London and, in fact, the flagon with such a cover is universally known among collectors as a 'beefeater' flagon.

From about 1675 onwards flagons were made in more varied styles, and begin to take on more originality in design.

The flat cover of the Stuart tankard was incorporated into the tall tapering cylindrical flagon, and in due course this was changed for the domed cover which came into fashion about the end of the 17th century. From then onwards the domed cover, either with or without a knop, or 'finial', became general, so far as English pewter flagons are concerned.

Fig. 65 shows a fine range of flagons of all periods from c.1610 onwards, in the collection of Mr. C. C. Minchin, of Reading. The first on the left of the top row being of c.1610; Nos. 3 and 7 in the top row; No. 4 in the second row, and No. 1 in the bottom row all being of c.1630.

The 'beefeater' is well represented in Nos. 2 and 6 in the top row. The late Stuart flat cover is shown in No. 8 (top), and in No. 3 (middle); these flagons can be dated as of c.1690–1700.

Of less uniform design are those shown at Nos. 5 (top), 1 (middle), and 2 and 3 (bottom), these range from c.1660 to c.1710.

No. 2 on the second shelf is an excellent example of a 'York' acorn-shaped flagon—so named because this type is found only in that area, and made by Yorkshire, or nearby, pewterers. This particular flagon is of *c*.1720–30.

English flagons after this date became again more stereotyped, and Fig. 64 shows good examples, dating from *c*.1725–45. A later flagon, of *c*.1750, is shown in Fig. 28.

There is only one main type which can be associated with Ireland, and this takes the general body form of the English 'beefeater' flagon, but has a domed cover and an extremely large and full-curved handle, quite unlike that seen on any other type. Irish flagons have not been found of date earlier than, say, 1740 or so, and they were made until, at least, the close of the century. The main differences in type of Irish examples lie in the incidence, or otherwise, of a spout. (See Fig. 66.)

In Scotland, too, the design can be said to be individual to that country. Here we find the tapering cylindrical drum, slightly incurved, and topped with a flat, or very shallow 'dished' cover.

Scottish flagons are almost always decorated with a wide band of reeding around the centre of the drum, and always have a plain single-curved handle. Examples of Scottish-type flagons are shown in Fig. 67. This type dates from *c*.1720 to *c*.1800.

Occasionally English pewterers made flagons to the Scottish pattern, notable among such makers being William Eden (or Eddon) of London, and Richard Going, of Bristol. The flagons illustrated being both by the latter maker.

Such flagons were, in all probability, made to special order for Scottish kirks.

Whereas a tall commodious flagon is, undoubtedly, the best vessel for dispensing the wine in a church where the communicants reach considerable numbers, there is no hard and fast rule which prescribes that the container shall be of any particular form or capacity. Several instances are on record of tankards, and even of tavern measures, having been used for this purpose, but in some areas this did not satisfy the visiting bishops, who, at Moreton, Essex (in 1683) ordered: 'The pewter Tankard to be changed for a ffaire fflagon', and in the same year, at Oakley Magna, Essex: 'The pewter Tankard that is for the use of the Communion must be changed for a fflagon'.[1]

Pewter patens, which were originally used for the reception of bread at the Lord's Supper, were quite frequently made in pewter, and, in their earliest known form, are small circular plates with deeply-cupped well and flat rim. Such is the shape of most of the patens found in 13th- and 14th-century tombs of ecclesiastics, but early plates, with very shallow depression, are also to be found but, from lack of precise knowledge, collectors have been unable to date them with any real degree of accuracy.

It is probable that the plate illustrated in Fig. 20 was intended as a paten, owing to its entire suitability for that purpose, and for acting as a stand for a flagon when not in use for the former purpose.

Many so-called patens, very probably, had no actual connection with the church at all, and are merely so named because their owners would like to think of them in that connection. In this category we can place many of the beautiful broad-rimmed plates of the mid-17th century, usually of between 9 and 10 inches in diameter.

Admittedly many were to be found in churches and, doubtless, were purchased for use as patens, but just as many would have served no higher purpose than as stands for flagons of the period, which, incidentally, are found to fit so neatly into the shallow well.

Something of this kind was particularly necessary with 17th-century flagons, which were not normally provided with a spout for clean pouring.

[1] *The Pewter Communion Vessels of Essex Churches*, The Rev. W. J. Pressey, M.A., F.S.A. 1927. p. 5.

Unless flagons, and other vessels, bear an engraved inscription, or there is other evidence which links them with a particular church, there is no sound reason for calling them church vessels at all.

Exactly similar types were made and used for domestic purposes.

It is conceivable that many of the footed plates of the late 17th and early 18th centuries were, in fact, made and used specifically for holding the Holy bread, and they can, thus, rightly be called patens. When known to have been purely domestic pieces they are more generally termed 'tazzae', or merely 'footed plates'. (See Fig. 68.)

Alms dishes in pewter were commonly used, and normally were identical with domestic pieces, but occasionally something more elaborate turns up, like the hammered and decorated example in Fig. 69.

There are other and rarer types of Alms dishes, with an enamel 'boss' in the centre, but genuine examples are scarce.

There is, however, a set of four such dishes belonging to the Church of St. Katherine Cree, in London; these dishes have radiating flutes beaten into the rim and booge, to add strength to the rim where it would receive the greatest amount of strain when filled with collected alms. Two of these dishes are still in the possession of the church, and the remaining pair may be seen at the Guildhall Museum, in London.

Font bowls are occasionally found in pewter, but there is, normally no feature which distinguishes them from normal household food bowls.

Cotterell illustrates two late 18th-century examples of deep bowls, still contained in their original wrought iron brackets, from Scottish churches.

Pewter Chrismatories are frequently mentioned in the records of the official visitations of Exeter churches in the early 14th century, as the following extracts will testify: at Sydebury (*sic*), (Sidbury), 13th July, 1301, there was found 'a Chrismatory of pewter, with a lock', and a similar piece at Culmstock, in the same area. At Colyton (14th July, 1330), 'there is a sufficiently good Chrismatory of pewter, with a lock', and, again, Chrismatories with locks were found at Littleham and Topsham during the same month.

We have little indication of their form or size; we know only that they were made of 'fine metal', as laid down by ordinance of the Pewterers' Company in 1348, and were then called 'Square Crismatories'.

No early English specimen in pewter has, so far, come to light.

Mention is made, in Chapter Five, of the use of candlesticks for church processional purposes in the early 14th century, but here again we have little detailed records as to their type. They were, it is thought, most probably of pricket form, and possibly followed the Continental styles, but one must not overlook the fact that our earliest known candlesticks in *pottery* were made with hollow candle holders, and that they took their form from the Venetians who, in turn, had 'borrowed' the design from the Persians.

There is no known pewter candlestick, either in private hands or in a museum, about which one could say, by reference to the design alone, that it was made specifically for either lay or secular purposes.

We cannot leave the subject of Church pewter without mention of the small 'tokens' issued by Scottish churches as an 'admission ticket' to those wishing to take Holy Communion.

The earliest tokens of the Presbyterian Church of Scotland appear to have been issued in the late 16th century, and were, originally, in lead, but very shortly pewter was adopted for their manufacture as being a more suitable material.

The first mention of pewter (or 'tin') tokens seems to be in the City of Glasgow in 1603.

These little items were made in two or three different ways; sometimes they were merely small flat pieces of lead or pewter, not more than 1 inch square, roughly cut to a particular shape, and punched with an iron stamp which bore a device, generally of the simplest character.

Others were made in moulds, very crudely prepared, of two plates of iron or stone, with the design incised on one half, and with a groove running out to the edge. When the two halves of the mould were placed together the groove formed a channel through which the molten metal was poured. Tokens made by this method were probably cast by the local Church-wardens as required, although the records show many instances of pewterers and whitesmiths being commissioned for the purpose.

Towards the end of the 18th century and well into the 19th century Communion tokens were struck from dies, in the same way as a medal is struck today.

BIBLIOGRAPHY

COTTERELL, H. H.: 'Fine Work of the York Pewterers', *Apollo*, July, 1933.
—— 'An Early Pewter Baptismal Bowl', *Antique Collector*, January, 1932.
—— 'A Pewter Ringer's Flagon', *Apollo*, March, 1933.
—— 'Treasures in the Scott Nicholson Collection', *Apollo*, February, 1934.
—— 'Saynt Povles Flagon', *Connoisseur*, April, 1929.
DE NAVARRO, ANTONIO: 'Pewter Church Flagons', *Country Life*, 9th January, 1909.
MICHAELIS, RONALD F.: 'Pear-shaped Flagons in Pewter', *Antique Collector*, October, 1961.
MINCHIN, CYRIL C.: 'Flagons and Tankards in Pewter', *Antique Collector*, February, 1952.
PRESSEY, W. J. Rev. *The Pewter Communion Vessels of Essex Churches*, reprinted from Trans. of the Essex Archaeol. Soc., Vol. XVIII, part 3, 1927.
SHELLEY, ROLAND J. A.: 'Inscriptions on Church Pewter Plate', *Apollo*, November, 1948.
SUTHERLAND GRAEME, A. V.: 'Pewter Church Flagons', *Connoisseur*, June, 1946.
—— 'Pewter Church Plate', *Connoisseur*, Part I, October, 1936; Part II, April, 1940.

CHAPTER EIGHT

MISCELLANEOUS OBJECTS IN PEWTER

THERE ARE MANY small and unusual items in pewter which a collector finds it difficult to assign to any particular group. There are, of course, pewter toys, which make a fascinating sideline to any collection, and when these can be displayed on a miniature dresser, or in a model kitchen, the effect is delightful.

Small pewter models of the more usual kitchen requisites have frequently been excavated when digging operations have taken place in the City of London, and the Guildhall Museum can show a small but representative collection of such items; also there were many pieces of doll's house kitchenware made in Victorian times.

Some 17th-century pewterers seem to have made a speciality of toy production, and several instances are on record of these men having disobeyed regulations and produced toys which did not fulfil the rigid standards of quality laid down by the Company's ordinances.

For example, on the 15th September, 1668, one Francis Lea was fined 10s. for producing 'his Toy Pestell and Mortar and other toyes at five grains (below standard)', and, in 1714, William Hux and another pewterer were admonished for making toy watch cases of the same poor quality. They were threatened with dismissal from the Company unless they improved their ware. At least one of William Hux's toy watch cases is known to be in a private collection, and there may be others extant.

Other small objects are pewter Tobacco Stoppers; Dog Whistles; Sugar Crushers, for use in glasses of hot rum or punch; Meat Skewers with ornamental heads, the prong often being reinforced with an iron core; Candle Snuffers with tray; and many more items, too numerous to mention.

Pewter Snuffboxes have been made in a wide variety of shapes and sizes from about the beginning of the 18th century, and they seem to have been produced until, at least, the middle of the 19th century. In many cases pewter boxes were made in exact replica of similar articles in silver—in fact, there can be little doubt that they were purposely made in this fashion for those persons who were unable to afford the price of snuffboxes in the rarer metal.

Some of the earlier specimens will show traces of gilding, either inside or out, or both; some even of coloured enamel or paint having been used to add emphasis to the design.

Many and varied are the shapes and sizes of these charming little boxes; the most fascinating probably being those fashioned into the shape of a shoe, or some other familiar object such as a double-barrelled flint-lock pistol.

It is possible that some of the more elongated types were intended for use as needlecases, but they serve equally well for either purpose. Others which, obviously, can serve a dual purpose are match boxes; these latter can be distinguished by a small panel of corrugated lines incorporated into the design, usually beneath the lid, but sometimes also on the base, upon which the vesta could be struck.

Since vestas came into general use only about the 1830's it is obvious that none of these can be of any great age.

It is unusual to find a pewter snuffbox with a maker's mark; one maker, however, whose mark does occasionally appear on English boxes is 'R. WEBSTER', used either in full, or in a small panel containing the initials R.W. only. There is no recorded information of this maker, but he is unlikely to have operated much before the end of the 18th century.

Snufftaking must have been a popular habit in Scotland, for, in addition to the large variety of horn and silver mulls from that country, we find a quantity of pewter, and pewter-mounted, mulls.

Many are made from complete cow or goat horns, with a pewter rim and a hinged cover, and others from the half hoof of a deer, and these are similarly mounted. (See Fig. 70.)

The name 'DURIE' may sometimes be found impressed on the underside of the lid, and although we have little information of this maker, it is recorded that he operated in the neighbourhood of Inverurie, probably during the first quarter of the 19th century.

The name 'CONSTANTINE' sometimes appears on another type of Scottish mull, composed entirely of pewter, but made in the semblance of a curled cow horn. These may be dated a little earlier, perhaps from the last quarter of the 18th century.

Tobacco stoppers were used for pressing down the half-smoked dottle in the bowl of clay pipes from, at least, c.1700, and specimens are found in a variety of shapes; that of a truncated leg, often with topboot or shoe attached, being, perhaps, the commonest.

Tobacco stoppers are often mistaken for seals, probably because of the flat end used for pressure against the tobacco, but the latter can usually be distinguished by the fact that the flat section is often larger than could be inserted into a pipe bowl—particularly the small bowled clays—and secondly they often bear initials engraved *in reverse* on the flat end.

When those ownership initials are cut the right way, and not in reverse, there can be no doubt that the object was intended as a stopper and not as a seal.

Collectors will, doubtless, come across pounce pots in a variety of styles. These conform very closely to the sort of thing we know as pepper pots today, and are often found in larger sizes, which might conceivably have been sugar casters.

It is quite likely that many were, in fact, made for use as

pepper casters but, apart from the size of the holes, there is little to distinguish the one from the other.

Fig. 71 shows a selection of pounce pots and pepper pots, mostly of baluster form, but includes two differing owl models. These have holes in the eyes and at the top of the head for pouring, and may be filled by unscrewing at the neck.

The pug dog in the same illustration is one of a pair, and is filled through a hole in the breast; this hole being sealed in use by a small cork or plug.

Pounce pots date from c.1730 onwards, and were used for pouring pounce (or fine sand) upon the wet ink after a letter was written.

The powder could then be shaken off the paper, and be poured back into the pot, or thrown away.

Cylindrical pounce pots, with the top drilled for shaking, may occasionally be found, but in all probability these will be the shakers that have become separated from the Standish (or Inkstand) of which they originally formed a part.

A late 17th-century type of standish was in the form of a shallow rectangular tray, often on raised, globular feet, and with the tray fitted with depressions into which round, turret-shaped pots for ink and pounce were kept. Sometimes these standishes are fitted with a drawer, or other receptacle, for quills and, perhaps, sealing wax, incorporated in the piece itself, and it is not unusual to find such tray-type inkstands also fitted with a holder for a taper or candle. The candle not only provided light for the scribe, but was also useful for melting the sealing wax with which many early documents were sealed.

The earliest known English pewter inkstand is that shown in Fig. 72 (a) and (b), which is illustrated by kind permission of the Governors of St. Bartholomew's Hospital. Upon the cover is inscribed 'The Guifte of Mr. Martin Bonnde' and the date '1619', together with a representation of the donor's

Arms. Martin Bond was Treasurer of St. Bartholomew's Hospital from 1620 to 1642.

Very few early full-lidded types of inkstands, such as this, have survived, but another popular type, with all the essential containers fitted inside was produced about the end of the 17th century, and similar examples were made throughout the 18th century. These have become known as 'Treasury' inkstands, a name said to be acquired from a silver example at that particular Government office. (See Fig. 13.) In pewter it was made in several sizes; the smallest being approximately 6¾ inches long by 4½ inches wide by 2 inches high. The largest which has come to the writer's notice measuring some 13 inches long, with other dimensions in proportion.

Another popular type of inkstand is the 'Capstan' type shown in Fig. 14, such pieces were made from about 1780 onwards, and are usually found with the broad base plate, as shown, but later examples have been made without it.

During the reigns of the Stuarts several coins were minted in pewter; for example there is a pewter Crown piece of Charles I, struck at Oxford in 1644, and at least one farthing each of Charles II, James II and William and Mary, and several halfpennies were struck, both in England and Ireland, in the reign of James II.

These coins were sometimes made with a small plug of copper pressed into them before the design was struck, probably as a deterrent to fakers, who would have found that to cast a soft pewter coin without the plug was an easy task, but not so easy when the two metals were combined.

All these pewter coins are rare and desirable when in good condition.

Many pewter tokens and medallions were produced during the reigns of the Georges and later, particularly in commemmoration of Coronations, and these make an interesting sideline to any collection.

Beggars' Badges have been made in pewter, both in

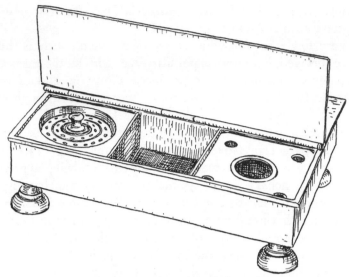

FIG. 13. Inkstand with hinged
cover, known as 'Treasury' type.

FIG. 14. Inkstand of 'Capstan', or 'Logger-
head' type, in use from the late 18th
century to well into the 19th century.

England, and Scotland, from the mid-16th century onwards—the first recorded instance in England known to the writer being in Gloucester in 1555–6, and, in Scotland, the first mention of their use appears in an Act of Parliament of 1424, wherein the sick and needy were ordained to be provided with, and ordered to wear, a leaden badge.

These badges take many forms, mostly being round and flat, with holes for hanging or stringing on to the clothing, and with the name of the issuing town, and a distinguishing number, impressed or cast upon the front surface; sizes vary from 1½ inches diameter to well over 3 inches, in some cases.

The recipient had to wear the badge in a prominent position or he would be made to suffer severe penalties, the reasons for such severity being to attempt to curtail the number of 'deceivable hawkers and beggars' who continually roamed the country, and to enable the really needy to be distinguished from such vagabonds.

The badge allowed the wearer free passage in and out of the gates of his city, and gave him the privilege of begging for alms within the walls.

Early specimens of these badges are rare, but late 18th- and early 19th-century Scottish badges turn up from time to time.

Readers are cautioned to beware of so-called Pilgrims' Badges, and other objects of pseudo-mediaeval interest, said to have been excavated in diggings in and around Thames-side, but which are, in reality, fakes of the worst kind—made in the semblance of seals, hanging badges, figurines of ecclesiastics and such like. These objects are cast in poor quality pewter and, sometimes, in lead and brass, and bear raised decoration depicting knights in armour, bishops and the like, and often have indecipherable and meaningless lettering round the edges with, perhaps, a 13th- or 14th-century date in *Arabic* numerals incorporated in the design.

Large numbers of these fakes were produced by a pair of rogues known as 'Billy & Charley', i.e. William Smith and

Charles Eaton, who had a workshop in the neighbourhood of
Rosemary Lane, Tower Hill, and during the middle years of
the 19th century produced many hundreds of these pieces,
which they then purported to have found in the mud banks
of the river.

The activities of these fakers were first exposed at a meeting
of the British Archaeological Association in 1858, by the late
Syer Cuming, who claimed to have examined over 800
examples of their work.

Fig. 74 shows examples of figurines, and also specimens of
vases displaying dates.

Certain old medical requisites were made in pewter, such as
Syringes, Invalids' Feeding Cups or 'Pap-boats', Infants'
Feeding Bottles, and Castor Oil Spoons. Bleeding bowls
with graduated markings inside the bowl, to measure the
amount of blood 'let' from the patient, have been dealt with
in another chapter.

Castor Oil spoons are quaint objects, and their method of
use frequently puzzles the owners. They consist of a spoon-
shaped bowl, with a hinged cover, and have a tubular stem;
the piece measures about 4½ inches overall.

The normal procedure is for the shaped bowl to be filled
with the requisite amount of oil, and then for the administrator
to place a fingertip over the hole at the end of the handle; the
spoon can then be tipped into the patient's mouth without
fear of spilling the liquid. When the finger is removed from
the hollow handle the air flow thus created allows the oil to
run out and into the mouth. The spoon would be warmed
over a flame before use to ensure an easy flow of the oil.

It is doubtful if such objects were made prior to the early
19th century.

Chimney ornaments in the shape of horses, dogs, pheasants,
or small human figures, made in flat form and placed upon
wide stepped bases, were made in pewter as well as brass
during the early 19th century. They were probably the

pewterers' answer to the Staffordshire potters who, about this time, were producing the pairs of pottery poodles and other mantel ornaments which were so popular with cottagers because of their low price.

All these 'bygones' are now becoming increasingly difficult to find, and in time many will become items for the serious collector.

One might say the same for the later Victorian tankards, which are so often neglected in this country.

In the United States of America, where pewtering continued for about a hundred years after it had begun to wane in England, these tankards are snapped up, and it may well be that English collectors of the future will have to go across the Atlantic to find further additions to their collections and, let it be admitted, at prices far in excess of those for which they can be bought today.

BIBLIOGRAPHY

COTTERELL, HOWARD H.: 'XVIIth Century Pewterers' Tokens', *Connoisseur*, May, 1927 and September, 1929.
—— 'Diminutive Pewter for Small Homes', *Antique Collector* (U.S.A.), Part I, April, 1932; Part II, July, 1932.

BROOK, ALEXANDER J.: 'Communion Tokens of the Established Church of Scotland', Proc. Soc. Ant. of Scotland, XLI (1907), pp. 453–648.

MACADAM, W. IVESON: 'Church Tokens of Various Parish Churches', Proc. Soc. Ant. of Scotland, XIV, pp. 163–9.

MICHAELIS, RONALD F.: 'Collecting Old Pewter Snuffboxes', *Apollo*, January, 1947.

PORT, CHARLES G. J.: 'Some Uncommon Pieces of Pewter', *Connoisseur*, Part I, April, 1917; Part II, December, 1917; Part III, October, 1918; Part IV, September, 1921; Part V, March, 1925.

SUTHERLAND GRAEME, A. V.: 'Some Uncommon Pewter Inkstands', *Country Life*, 8th October, 1948.
—— 'Old Pewter Snuffboxes', *Bazaar, Exchange and Mart*, 2nd November, 1937.

CHAPTER NINE

DECORATION ON PEWTER

ENGLISH PEWTERWARE generally may be said to be conspicuous by the absence of purely ornamental decoration upon its surface; most of it relying solely on good design and excellent workmanship and metal for its lasting qualities.

With this fact well established in mind from our textbooks, it may come as a surprise to some collectors to realize to what extent English pewter from the best period, i.e. the 17th century, deviates from this path of rectitude and displays remarkably fine applied decoration, either in the form of 'wriggled-work' engraving or cast ornamentation.

Wriggled-work decoration is contrived by the engraver who, having selected a tool with a narrow chisel-like blade, holds this at an angle and pushes it across the metal, at the same time rocking the blade from side to side, thereby chipping out small particles of the surface by each movement of the tool. Considerable skill can be displayed in practice, and pewterers frequently made use of this method.

Normal line engraving was found to be not so effective, firstly because the metal, being soft in comparison with silver or latten, did not stand up to the deep cutting necessitated by the latter method, and secondly, again because of its comparative softness, the cuts soon became smooth, and even when filled up with dirt and discolouration failed to remain visible for any length of time. An excellent example of wriggled-work is shown on the flat-lidded Stuart tankard in Fig. 75. This process was used prolifically by mid- to late 17th-century pewterers and others up to, at least, the end of the first quarter of the 18th century.

Numerous plates and dishes, by known London makers,

exist in private collections; many of them being in pairs and intended, originally, as Marriage Commemorative plates. (See Fig. 76.)

Engraving on pewter is first mentioned in the Pewterers' Company records in 1588, when one Andrew Bowyer was fined 2s., 'for that he set a stranger to work to grave uppon his pewter when he might have it wrought by a brother of the Company'. About eighteen months later this pewterer was again in trouble for a similar offence; the entry (of 14th January, 1590) reading: 'Whereas Andrew Bowyer hath heretofore been admonished for setting to work a woman to grave uppon his pewter, contrary to the ordinances of the house, and hath payed his fine for it, he is again charged for the like offence and is adjudged to pay 5s. fine, with a threat of the maximum fine of three pounds for a further offence.'

From these entries it is clear that the pewterers themselves were normally responsible for adding the engraved decoration to pewterware, and this no doubt accounted for the crudity, so frequently displayed, in the workmanship of the designs employed.

It was not to be expected that these simple metal workers could readily turn their hands to intricate artistic decoration with the same degree of competence as trained engravers. In fact, it is this very simplicity and crudity of execution which lends such charm to most of their work, and one could make an extremely interesting specialized collection of pewter pieces bearing such adornment.

Another, though little used, method of decoration was by punched ornamentation. To achieve this a series of shaped punches, or dies, was used; the dies being made of steel, the ends tooled or cut in high relief with an ornamental design, such as a semi-circle or crescent; a tudor rose; a fleur-de-lys, or some other purely conventional motif.

The design was built up by the use of several of these

punches, struck repeatedly to form a running ornamentation round the border of plates and dishes.

An excellent example is illustrated in Fig. 78 which shows the repeated use of two separate dies for the main pattern, and with an additional die of a rose to separate the date and the ownership initials at the top.

These designs were implanted on the metal in exactly the same way as the pewterers' touch, itself, was struck, i.e. by a sharp blow of a hammer upon the reverse end of the die, thus forcing the matrix of the die into the soft metal.

The specimen illustrated is dated (also by the use of punches) '1585', and bears the ownership initials 'M.A.' and 'M.B.'.

A very similar dish, 12⅝ inches diameter, with punched marginal decoration is at the British Museum, bearing the same date, i.e. 1585, and the names 'IONE✤COPPEN✤ SVSAN✤CHVRCH'.

These dishes appear to be either betrothal or marriage commemorative pieces.

The traditional process of manufacture of most items of pewter hollow-ware was by the casting of the component parts in moulds made especially for the purpose. It is only a short step onwards for the craftsman to engrave (or cut and gouge) the insides of these moulds, thereby creating the matrices from which decoration on the cast article would stand out in bold relief.

It is ornamentation of the latter character which appears on some of our finest specimens of 16th- and 17th-century pewter; why it was not used more frequently is difficult to fathom, and it must be supposed that ornamentation *of any sort*, being foreign to our pewterers' conception of art, was discouraged by the powers governing the fraternity.

The William Grainger candlestick (dated 1616), now in the possession of the Victoria and Albert Museum, is the most celebrated example of relief cast pewter (see Fig. 79), and there is another exceptional dated item, though not by any means so well known, in the form of a footed plate or Paten, at the Church of St. Mary's, West Shefford, Berks.

The author is indebted to Mr. Cyril C. Minchin, of Reading, for excellent photographs of this treasure, which are reproduced herewith. (See Figs. 81 (a) and (b).)

This tazza comprises a shallow bowl or dish, mounted on a moulded and knopped stem, with a domed foot ornamented with daisies, roses and birds, in high relief.

The centre of the bowl bears the figure of a knight in armour carrying a lance, his charger fully caparisoned. Around the centre medallion is the legend:

'WHAT★HAVE★WE★THAT★WE★HAVE★NOT★
RECEIVED★OF★THE★LORD'

and the date '1616'.

The rim is enriched by a belt of sixteen plain shields bearing respectively: three lions passant; St. Andrew's cross; three fleurs de lys; a chevron between three roses; a lion rampant; a cross gules, in the dexter canton a dagger; a stringed harp; a chevron between three strikes (ingots of tin), upon the chevron three roses—these are the arms of the Pewterers' Company. Of these the lions of England, the Scottish lion, the Irish harp, the Arms of the City of London, St. Andrew's cross and the chevron between three roses each occur twice; the fleur de lys of France three times, and the Pewterers' Arms only once.

On the plain surround, outside the centre boss, is engraved:

'THE★GIFTE★OF★THOMAS★HARVYE★IN★
AN°★D°★1621★MARCH★31'.[1]

No English pewter of this type known to the writer can be ascribed with certainty to a period earlier than that of James I, although the footed cup shown in Fig. 80 could quite easily

---

[1] This tazza is recorded and illustrated in *The Church Plate of Berkshire*, by J. W. & M. I. Walker, 1927, p. 261.

have originated in the previous reign. It has certain Elizabethan features but, being undated, its precise date must
remain conjectural.

We are more fortunate in our three following examples,
Fig. 82 shows a beaker ornamented with conventional scrolls
of grape vines and roses, with an occasional bloom which
can be likened to a daisy or marigold. The wider band of
decoration at the top has as its main motifs, in circular cartouches, the Rose and Crown of England, and the Prince of
Wales's feathers flanked by the initials 'H' and 'P' (for
Henricus Princeps).

These initials, combined with the feathers of Bohemia, can
relate only to Henry Frederick, son of James I of England, who
was created Prince of Wales in 1610. Prince Henry was born
in 1594, and even at an early age showed promise of rivalling
his father in the favouritism of the Court. At the age of
fifteen or thereabouts he was installed in his own quarters at
St. James's Palace, London, and it is thought that this beaker was
one of, perhaps, a number made for everyday use in the Royal
household.

The Prince of Wales died of typhoid fever in 1612 and, thus,
the beaker can be dated between the years of his succession to
the title in 1610 and the year of his death in 1612. An identical
beaker is in the collection of Mr. C. C. Minchin, of Reading.

The beaker shown in Fig. 83 is smaller than the previous
item, being only $4\frac{5}{8}$ inches high, with a capacity of about
8 fluid oz (i.e. about $\frac{1}{2}$ pint, Old English Wine Standard), and
varies from the former in the formation of the foot flange,
which is of solid metal. This foot, however, is (in the
writer's opinion) not original.

The bands of relief casting are of similar conventional
design to those on the former beaker, but in this case the
central band bears the Prince of Wales's feathers repeated twice,
and interspaced with the Arms of the Stuarts in garter, and also
the Rose and Crown.

The decoration is somewhat worn by usage and cleaning, and if the initials of the young Prince were ever incorporated these have long since disappeared.

In this case one must assume that the beaker, being so nearly similar in style of decoration, also commemorates Prince Henry, although there is the possibility that Prince Charles (later Charles II) could be indicated. Charles was created Prince of Wales in 1638 at the age of eight years, and was granted his own establishment in that year.

Fig. 85 shows a beaker of differing type, but with a still more glorious array of Royal Stuart emblems. The Prince of Wales's feathers appear four times in the top band of decoration, and at the centre are circlets containing the Rose and Crown and the Stuart Arms. In four semi-circular cartouches just below the central band of adornment are representations of the Thistle, the Rose and the Fleur-de-lys. There can be little doubt that this, too, can be attributed to the period of James I.

Yet another beaker with cast decoration is illustrated (Fig. 84), and there seems every justification for dating it closely with that in Fig. 82.

It is of almost identical size, style and shape, and it also bears bands of running ornament encircling the drum; the foot, too, is similarly decorated.

Immediately below the lip are two circlets of wording, reading: 'TO DRINK AND BE MERRYE IS NOT AMISS —AND WITH THY FRED (Friend) ABIDE—THY MIRTH AND DRINKING (MUST) TAKE HEED THOU DOEST NOT (CHIDE) R.B.'. This treasure is at the London Museum, having been found, with other objects of coeval date, in a cellar of a house in old Cheapside.

The plate, or shallow dish, shown in Fig. 86 was dug up in Norton Folgate, London, and is now also to be found at the London Museum.

It is shown here so that the reader may have an opportunity of comparing photographs of all known styles of cast decorated

17th-century pewter. In all probability this particular piece was made for use as a flagon stand; the foot of the flagon fitting in the deep groove around the centre boss.

So far as is known no other writer has drawn attention to relief casting as an essential feature of English pewter of the early 17th century, although, from time to time, examples of such decoration in use as medallions in the bowls of pewter porringers have been noted.

Cotterell illustrates two examples of two-eared porringers in his *Old Pewter, its Makers and Marks* (Plate LXI), and a further specimen is shown in Fig. 88. This porringer bears a medallion depicting William III, and it can, thus, be dated fairly accurately.

William of Orange, and Mary, daughter of James II, ascended the English throne in 1688, and they reigned jointly until 1694, when Mary died of smallpox. William III continued to reign alone until 1702, and since he is depicted here without his Queen it seems reasonable to suppose that this particular piece was made between the years 1694 and 1702. In any event, it was certainly made during his reign as sovereign, for the initials 'W' and 'R' appear, one on either side of the head—the 'W' surmounted by a Crown, and the 'R' by an Orb.

In addition, there is, on the reverse of one ear, a maker's mark which can be attributed to one Samuel Lawrence, of London, a pewterer who became 'free' on 22nd March, 1687.

Porringers with bossed centres of Royal portrait busts, and others illustrating historical events, such as the Peace of Ryswick, with the Duke of Marlborough in evidence, are known, but are exceedingly rare. All such pieces seem to date from around 1688 to the end of the reign of Queen Anne.

One other type of cast decorated porringer, or wine taster, is shown at Fig. 87. This is only 2⅞ inches in bowl diameter, and so the latter appellation is probably correct. This has a centre boss depicting the five-petalled Tudor Rose, and has a relief cast ear incorporating the initials 'C.R.'. The initials are, in all probability, intended to indicate Charles Rex, i.e. Charles I or, perhaps, Charles II (the latter seems more likely in view of the general style of the piece itself). They could, of course, represent the maker, although it is unusual for pewterers to mark their wares in this way.

This particular specimen is in a private collection, but an identical example is housed in the Victoria and Albert Museum, where it is dated (in the writer's opinion, quite correctly) as of mid-17th-century period.

Perhaps the most popular group of cast decorated pewter is that containing spoons of the late 17th and early 18th centuries, bearing Royal portraits of reigning sovereigns. The earliest identifiable portraits are of William III and Mary, c.1688–94, although specimens have come to light which may well represent Charles II or James II, but which, in the writer's opinion, are more likely to portray William III alone. Such specimens would date from c.1694 to 1702.

There is a prolific range of spoons bearing a portrait of Queen Anne; only one or two of the castings bearing any true resemblance to this somewhat buxom character. In all specimens the Queen is found facing to the left, with flying angels at each side of the head, holding aloft a Royal Crown. On some appear the initials 'A.R.', for Anne Regina.

Spoons of otherwise similar type, but without Royal portraits, were popular in Holland and other parts of the Continent at the turn of the 17th century, and it is probable that the vogue for cast ornamentation on spoons originated there. In Continental examples, however, the decoration consists of purely decorative designs of a heart, or an urn-shaped vase, surrounded by elaborate floreate scrolls. Somewhat similar types were made by English pewterers.

The only other Royalty to be depicted in this way are George III and his Queen, Charlotte Sophia, of Mecklenburg Strelitz, whom he married in 1761, who appear on Hanoverian pattern spoons of the period. All known specimens (and at least three differing castings are known) were made by one John Vaughan, of London, whose marks appear on the reverse of the stem. (See Fig. 89[v].)

The examples of pewterware mentioned above depend solely on cast decoration for their attractiveness, but quite often the decoration is purely ancillary to the piece itself. Cast decoration, at its best, is used in this way, for example in the finely cast handles of the early cup shown in Fig. 24, and in drum mouldings of flagons and tankards.

BIBLIOGRAPHY

COTTERELL, H. H.: 'Decoration on Old English Pewter', *Antique Collector,* 15th July, 1931.

COTTERELL, H. H., and VETTER, R. M.: 'Decorated, or "Show" Pewter', *Apollo Magazine*, Part I, November, 1933; Part II, January, 1934; Part III, October, 1935; Part IV, April, 1936.

MICHAELIS, RONALD F.: 'Decoration on English Pewterware', in four parts, *Antique Collector*, October, 1963, February, August and December, 1964.

CHAPTER TEN

MAKERS' MARKS

THE PRACTICE of marking pewter with a distinguishing mark, for one purpose or another, has doubtless been in vogue since pewterware itself was made. From the earliest times the Pewterers' Company in London took upon itself the task of compelling its members to place their own mark, or touch, upon all wares made by them, so that each piece might be known from henceforth as the work of a particular maker.

As has been mentioned in earlier chapters, it was necessary for all pewterware to be made of a specific quality of metal according to the class of ware concerned, and severe penalties were meted out to offenders.

Searchers were appointed whose sole task it was to ensure that pewterers—not only in London, but in towns and villages far afield from the capital—maintained the high standards set up in London and that the men employed in the craft carried on the trade with honour towards their customers. This diligent control ensured the high reputation in which early English pewter was held in this country and abroad.

When faulty pewter was seized it was customary for it to be disfigured with a mark which, in 1474 at any rate, we know to have been in a certain form. In this year the records mention 'a poncheon of iron *with a brode arowe hede*' for the forfeit mark, and the same iron is again included in an inventory of the Company's goods in 1489.

As Mr. Welch himself has stated, 'it was doubtless the fate of all vessels marked with the broad arrow to be forfeited and melted down without delay, and it is not probable that any

example so marked is now procurable as a treasured specimen
by the collector of old pewter'.[1]

Other marks were used by the Company for special purposes, and a further example occurs in 1492, when the records
show a payment made 'for iiij new markyng irons for hollow-
ware men'. The records do not disclose either the purpose of,
or the device upon, these irons. They are more explicit,
however, in 1509 when was bought 'a markyng Iren of the
strake of Tin and the lillepot'.

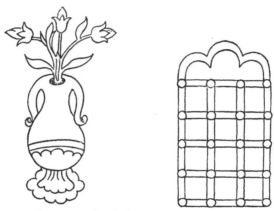

FIG. 15. The 'Lilypot' and the 'Strake',
copied from the margin of the Grant of Arms
to the Worshipful Company of Pewterers.

This device incorporates two emblems which have long
been associated with the Company; the 'lilypot' and the
'strike', or 'strake', of tin are both illustrated in the beautifully
illuminated Grant of Arms to the Company, dated 1533, and
the accompanying illustrations are reproduced from the margin
of the Grant.

To again quote Welch: 'This marking iron must have been
for official use, and was probably employed to denote good
quality, just as the broad arrow was used for the forfeit mark.
The entry is interesting for the light it throws on the nature of

[1] Welch, Vol. I, p. 47.

the "strakes" which are charges in the Company's Coat of Arms. From the delineations there given they would appear to be ingots of tin, although the object of piercing them in so many places, and with such regularity, is not at all clear.'.[1]

There is one further mention of an official mark, adopted in 1548, which throws some light on its purpose, and this is 'a markynge Iron of the flowre delyce (fleur de lys) to amarked (sic) stone pots with'. It is made clear in later entries that the pewter covers to stone pots had to be appraised and marked, for which service, in 1553-4, one of the Officials was granted 'one farthing for each dozen stone pots (with pewter lids) which were brought to him to mark at the Hall', and in 1556 it was agreed 'that Harry Tompson should have the vewe and markinge of all stone pots, and to mark only those substantially wrought. And for his painstaking in the same he should have his house rent free until further order'.

It is interesting to note that five years later, i.e. in 1558, the Court ruled that Harry Tompson was no longer to have the view and marking of stone pot lids, and from henceforth the mark of the Hall should not be put upon the lids. It was, however, an earlier injunction that the makers were to set their own marks *inside* the lid, and that the mark of the Hall should be set upon the *outside*. The order, in its amended form, provided that only the maker's mark was to appear, and that on the inside of the lid, as formerly.

The mark of the fleur-de-lys is, obviously, a simplification of the lily blossom which appears in the 'lilypot' previously drawn, and it is thought that the very adoption of the fleur-de-lys (as a quality mark) clearly establishes that the mark of the Lilypot, formerly mentioned, was also for quality.

There was at least one further official mark, and this was the Rose and Crown. This mark had long been associated with quality, and its promiscuous use was strictly forbidden by the Company.

[1] Welch, Vol. I, p. 99.

An entry of 1572 states that 'no man shall give for his proper touch the Rose and Crown, with letters or otherwise, but only him to whom it was given by the fellowship'. About 100 years later, in 1671 to be exact, it was agreed 'that from henceforth no person or persons whatsoever shall presume to strike the Rose and Crown with any additional flourish or the letters of his own or anothers name, whereby the mark *which is only to be used for goods exported*, may in time become as other touches and not distinguished'.

Within twenty years of this edict, however, the use of the Rose and Crown became more general, and it was used as a complementary mark by most London, and some provincial, pewterers.

An Order of 17th December, 1690, states that none shall strike any other mark upon his ware than 'his own proper touch and the Rose and Crown stamp'.

Throughout it has been established that the Rose and Crown should be accepted as a mark denoting the highest quality of pewterware, and not only by edict of the Company. An Act of Parliament passed in the reign of Charles I (1641) for regulating the makers of pewterware in Scotland states: 'It is ordained that the pewterer or founder of tin shall put the mark of the Thistle and the Deacon's mark with his own name upon every piece that he shall happen to cast, and that the same shall be *of the finest pewter, marked with the Rose in England* . . .'.

Before dealing with the pewterers' individual touches, it may be as well to mention a final mark which is found, as a complementary mark, on much late 17th- and 18th-century pewter.

Reference is here made to the Crowned letter 'X', as shown in the accompanying illustration.

In the first instance the use of this mark was strictly controlled by the Company, and the first mention of it appears to be in 1696, where it is ordained that: '. . . the letter X only to be stamped on Extraordinary ware, commonly called Hard Mettle'.

There is no doubt that for some considerable time due observance was paid to the governing order, for we frequently find the mark on good hard metal plates and dishes. In time, however, its use was abused, and it is found today on many Victorian tavern measures and tankards which cannot possibly lay honest claim to quality of metal or workmanship.

On the Continent the mark represented the alloy of tin and lead in the proportions of ten to one, and such may have been the original intention in this country. It is feasible that the symbol 'X' was intended to have the same significance as the Roman numeral.

Pewterers themselves had, doubtless, used a system of marking their wares with some distinguishing device long before it became compulsory for them to do so. In 1503–4 a most important Statute, 19 Henry VII (Cap. 7), lays down that 'all makers of pewter ware shall marke the same wares with severall marks of their owne, with the intent that the wares shall be avowed by them as truly wrought', and from henceforth the Pewterers' Company archives record a succession of infringements and punishments meted out to craftsmen who failed to observe the Act in whole or in part.

It is not until 1550 that any mention occurs of 'a table of pewter with every mans' mark thereon'. This is the first record of anything resembling a touchplate, which, of course, must have been a necessary record so soon as pewterers adopted a mark which was, from thenceforth, to be their personal 'trade mark'.

This 'table', and any other touchplates which may have been in use up to the time of the Great Fire of London, were presumably destroyed in that conflagration, when the Pewterers' Hall itself was burnt down, and these records are lost to us for ever.

Those of the pre-fire London pewterers who had survived

the plagues and the burning were required to restrike their marks on a new touchplate which was provided in the rebuilt Hall in 1667 or 1668, and the Company has in its possession today five touchplates, bearing in all some 1,090 marks used by London craftsmen from c.1640 to the present day.

The regulations required that every pewterer, upon the termination of his apprenticeship, and before setting up in business for himself, should prove his ability by the production of a 'trial piece', and, if found satisfactory (and provided he had the requisite capital), was granted 'leave to open and strike touch'.

The five existing London touchplates are illustrated in various published works, e.g. Welch's *History of the Worshipful Company of Pewterers*; Massé's *Pewter Plate*, second edition; and the late H. H. Cotterell's *Old Pewter, its Makers and Marks*, and it is assumed that readers will be able to gain access to one or another of these works, if reference to the plates is desired.

It can be said, however, that the first of the existing plates was brought into use in 1667, and that the first forty or so touches are those of pewterers who had, undoubtedly, been in business before the fire, and had been required to restrike their marks as and when they could get to the Hall to do so.

Following these we have a succession of marks of pewterers who had newly been granted freedom, but occasionally, interspersed with them, another old mark is struck.

It is this, apparently, haphazard collection of marks which seems to have puzzled the earlier writers, such as Welch and Massé, but Cotterell was able to 'bring order out of chaos', and his findings (as published in 1929) are now universally accepted.

Having decided *why* some early marks, dating from 1640 onwards, came to be struck on a touchplate which we now know to have been brought into use in 1667, the rest was comparatively easy going.

Whereas, hitherto, it had been possible to attribute only about one half of the marks from the first touchplate to known pewterers, we now know the owners of about 95 per cent. of these marks, and research is continually going on to establish the balance.

Generally speaking, it may be said that the earlier marks are from small circular punches, of initials or some simple device, contained in a beaded outline, but by the beginning of the 18th century the marks tended to be larger, and to contain more elaborate emblems, and frequently had their owner's Christian name and surname in full.

The marks which were struck upon the touchplates were from the main punches used by the craftsmen concerned, but upon their wares are often to be found additional marks such as the Rose and Crown; the Crowned X; a 'label' which, in some cases, might read 'Made in London' or 'Superfine Hard Metal', or, perhaps might even quote the pewterer's business address. In addition, there is sometimes to be found a sequence of four small punches, very like silver hallmarks; in fact, these latter were so often deliberately made to imitate silver hallmarks that the Goldsmiths' Company felt they had cause to complain of their use on several occasions.

These so-called hallmarks are usually to be found upon the brim of 17th-century plates and dishes, and the main touch, with or without supplementary marks, upon the back. In many cases the makers' initials appear in one or more of the hallmarks, and this is often of assistance in helping to decide the name of the maker—particularly when some of the other marks may have been imperfectly struck, or have been worn away by constant cleaning.[1]

It was not unusual for pewterers to have more than one touching iron—one of large size for large pieces, and a smaller iron, sometimes with less detail, for smaller wares such as spoons, salts and similar pieces.

Instances will be found of an item of pewterware bearing the marks of two distinct pewterers—perhaps the main touch of one and the hallmarks of another—and in such a case it may

[1] The first reference to such marks in the Pewterers' Company records is in 1635/6.

be assumed that the piece was made by a pewterer who, perhaps, specialized in that particular type of article, and who would be required to strike his own main touch upon it, and that it was made for sale by another pewterer who, probably, did not possess the moulds required in its manufacture.

There was, so far as we know, no obligation on the part of the second pewterer to place any mark of his own upon the ware, but it was natural that he should wish to do so, and his 'hallmarks' alone would suffice to show his interest in the finished article, and serve as his advertisement in the eyes of his customers.

The fact that pewterers traded between themselves is well documented throughout the records of the Company, as the following two instances, picked at random, will show. In 1581 the Court ordered that *none of the Company shall put to make any spoons but unto a brother of the Company*, and, in 1595, two pewterers, by name Humfrey Weetwood and Thomas Cowes, were admonished for making ear dishes (porringers), beakers, and 'godderdes' of false metal, and they were commanded to make satisfaction *unto the pewterers in the country who bought them from either of them*.

Other instances of dual marking can be accounted for by a business association, or by the succession of one pewterer to the business of another—such a case which comes readily to mind is that of Thomas Swanson, of London, whose main touch is frequently found with the 'hallmarks' of Samuel Ellis, also of London.

On some of Swanson's plates we even find a shaped 'label' bearing the words *Successor to S. Ellis, London*, which sets all doubts at rest.

Despite the stringent regulations that all pewterware should be marked with the maker's touch it is surprising how many items are found which bear no sign of a mark; in a few cases, of course, it is obvious that the mark has been detrited through constant cleaning and scouring, but in those cases it is unusual if some vestige of the mark does not still remain. In other cases the very condition of the piece will clearly show that no mark could ever have been struck upon it.

Whilst it is of inestimable benefit to find a maker's mark, and to be able to say with certainty that the piece was made by so and so, at a given date, or during a known period, it is strongly urged that collectors do not turn down good pewter because it bears no discernible mark. There are many other ways of dating pewter, either by its form or ornamental characteristics or, perhaps, by the amount of oxidization upon it.

Constant recourse to books of reference, and to private and public collections of pewter, should in time, enable one to form a very close estimate of the period and provenance of any particular item which may come to hand.

BIBLIOGRAPHY

BISSET, LT.-COL. J. S.: 'The Edinburgh Touchplates', *Antique Collector*, September, 1939.

COTTERELL, H. H.: 'Pewterers' Trade Tokens of the XVIIth Century', *Connoisseur*, May, 1927, and September, 1929.

COTTERELL, H. H., and HEAL, SIR AMBROSE: 'Pewterers' Trade Cards', *Connoisseur*, December, 1926, and February, 1928.

The London Touchplates are illustrated in photogravure (actual size) in:

Welch's *History of the Worshipful Company of Pewterers*, 1902.
Massé's *Pewter Plate*, 2nd ed., 1911.
Cotterell's *Old Pewter, its Makers and Marks*, 1929.

CHAPTER ELEVEN

ON COLLECTING

THE COLLECTORS of antique pewter have been less fortunate,
in some respects, than have been the collectors of fine porcelain,
glass, silver, furniture or even of more humble items such as
'bygones' in general. There is far less good collectable pewter
to be found than of contemporary articles in other media, and
one reason, of course, is that pewter, in spite of—or perhaps
because of—its very prevalence in its heyday, was not thought
to be of sufficient merit to warrant its retention for posterity.

As pewter began to be superseded by fine glazed pottery
and porcelain for table use it was relegated, first to the kitchen
dresser and, later, when servants became tired of perpetual
cleaning, to the attics.

The metal, by its very nature, lends itself to many modern
uses, and with the influx of canned foods, for example, the tin
content was needed for rendering the iron surface of the cans
impervious to the action of acids and corrosion.

Tin has many other uses, and scrap metal merchants have
been wont to pay fairly high prices for pewter articles for
melting down.

Within living memory there have been two World Wars,
during which the authorities have exhorted owners to scour
their attics and cellars for scrap metal of every kind, and,
through lack of knowledge and appreciation of such old things,
tremendous quantities of valuable old pieces have been sold
by weight for a few shillings per pound, and are lost to us
for ever.

The shortage of early American pewter, for instance, is put
down to the need for metal from which to cast bullets during
the War of Independence.

In addition to this perpetual drainage, the pewterers, them-selves, had a system of requiring their customers, where possible, to return old and damaged pewter for re-melting when orders were placed for new garnishes.

Bearing all these facts in mind it is the more surprising that so much has survived. One may argue that were it yet more prevalent it would be less desirable, and we must be thankful that it is still possible to form a representative collection of pewter items used in most walks of life from, at least, the late 17th century to the middle of the Victorian era.

The most likely objects to come the way of the beginner in the first instance are plates and dishes; and when these are in good condition, and of pleasing proportions, they make an excellent background for the miscellaneous pieces which will, doubtless, be acquired as knowledge increases, or as taste dictates.

In these days of flat-dwellers and small householders it is possible that the formation of a collection will be limited by the amount of space available for display, or again, if one is going to specialize in particularly early or rare pieces, then the limitation will be dictated by the pocket, but whatever the circumstances, it will be as well to come to an early decision on the form the collection is to take, and then to keep one's eyes open for pieces which fit into the scheme one has outlined. This all sounds a very simple and methodical way of procedure, and it is unlikely that any collection will conform to the predestined pattern for very long, simply because the very thing one looks for, and hopes to find, very rarely turns up. In the course of the search other things will be seen and bought because of their aesthetic appeal, and when one has the true collector's outlook it is not easy to deny oneself the pleasure of acquisition.

In most fields of collecting the supply of old pieces very rarely equals the demand, and so the fakers have given their attention to the production of objects made especially to deceive the unwary. No less is this the case with pewter, and the beginner will require to have his wits about him when he is offered supposedly rare pieces at prices too tempting to refuse.

The connoisseur knows that the chance of finding a real treasure at a bargain price crops up only once or twice in a lifetime, and that most of his best pieces have been acquired the hard way.

This may seem to be a cynical outlook, but better to tread warily, and make haste slowly, than go headlong into a buying expedition just to make a show which is thought to eclipse the more carefully selected display of a collector acquaintance.

Friendly rivalry in collecting is excellent when one reaches the stage of discretion and discrimination, but in the meantime it behoves one to handle, examine and study as much pewter as possible in all quarters; to read all the available literature on the subject, and to take the advice of knowledgeable friends until a feeling of confidence is acquired.

It is almost certain that mistakes will be made, but provided one learns by them, and avoids the pitfalls on subsequent occasions, no harm will be done. In fact, it is well to retain for frequent examination any pieces which have been proved to be fakes, and to compare these critically with good pieces of the same type when, or if, they turn up.

Naturally, the pieces most likely to be faked are what would, normally, be the rarest or most desirable types, such as early candlesticks, tapersticks, salts, Stuart flat-lidded tankards, early flagons, broad-brim plates and dishes, and pieces which bear commemorative dates or other engraving.

The experienced collector knows that tin, which forms the major ingredient of good pewter, acquires a film of oxidization after exposure to the elements for a number of years, and that the true oxidization and 'tinpest' which attacks old metal cannot be adequately faked. When one is able to recognize the true 'age' on a piece of pewter the battle is more than half won, but there will always turn up old pieces which have been so ruthlessly cleaned that all traces of this deterioration have been eliminated, and these will often remain 'puzzle pieces', even for the experts. There should, nevertheless, be some feature in the making or quality which will distinguish them from reproductions. Old metal, when recast, loses a certain porosity, and it takes on a different appearance and feel for those able to appreciate the difference.

When an old and corroded specimen has been cleaned with acid, and all traces of the deposit have been removed, there is left a surface which may be pitted or roughened to a greater or less extent, and only continual examination of such pieces during the process of cleaning will enable one to recognize the effects of such treatment.

The fakers know more about this than most collectors, and they have attempted to give to their productions some semblance of the correct appearance, but the *exact* symptoms *cannot* be reproduced, simply because the basic metal is no longer the same after re-melting and re-modelling.

Most of the fakes now on the market were produced during the years 1910 to 1930, or thereabouts, when collectors were prepared to pay high prices for rare and unusual items. Before the early years of the 20th century there were practically no books of reference on pewter and, consequently, very few collectors, but with the publication of Welch's *History of the Pewterers' Company*, in 1902, and Ingleby Wood's *Scottish Pewterware and Pewterers*, in 1907, interest in the subject grew rapidly and, in the following years, several exhibitions of pewter were staged, and more was written by the late H. J. L. J. Massé and others. By the year 1910 competition among collectors was keen, and prices for fine pieces began to soar to unforeseen heights. This was the cue for unscrupulous dealers to cash in on the demand, and their productions have now acquired some forty years or so of legitimate age. This makes them all the more difficult of detection today, and what was able to deceive collectors then must be examined far more critically now.

Enough should have been said to put collectors on their guard, and it is hoped that none will be discouraged by the possible pitfalls.

For those whose taste or pocket guides them into the realms of mid-18th century and later pewter there is little to worry about.

Such items have not yet been considered of sufficient importance to warrant reproduction on any large scale, and the collector can proceed with confidence.

Having acquired a few pleasing pieces the enthusiast will give his mind to the question of adequate display and, generally speaking, there is no more suitable medium for this purpose than old oak furniture.

There are few things more delightful than the glint of firelight on pewter spaced attractively round the room, in company with an old Welsh dresser and, perhaps, a carved mantelpiece surround, both of which give the right atmosphere for display. Narrow shelf fixtures at picture-rail level make an excellent additional feature, and can be used for the smaller pieces, with plates and dishes for background.

For spoons it is occasionally possible to find an old oak or elm spoon-rack which does not take up too much wall space, and really shows off pewter spoons in the right setting. Most racks will take about a dozen spoons, mostly hanging stem downwards, but if a rack can be found which allows spoons to hang with the ornamental knops upwards they are then seen to the best advantage.

Often the container, or knife box, at the foot of the rack will allow small pieces, such as salts or snuffboxes, also to be shown.

Sooner or later there will arise the question of whether pewter should be highly cleaned or left in its dull grey condition, and the decision must necessarily rest on the individual choice of the collector. Enough has been said in the last few pages to point out the dangers of *over-cleaning* specimens, and owners will, doubtless, aim at some intermediate stage of brightness.

Purists will say that pewter, when in use, was kept brightly scoured and free from dirt and grease, in the same way as kitchen pottery is kept today—but pewter is of a very different nature from pottery in that its surface takes on a fine sheen from continuous careful polishing, and forms a skin of patination very akin to that on old furniture similarly treated.

No one in his right senses would advocate stripping down a piece of antique furniture to its original bare wood surface, and, in the writer's view, it would be sacrilege to treat antique pewter in such a way that all traces of its acquired age were removed.

By all means clean off the ugly and detrimental corrosion which attacks the metal, but in the process ensure that sufficient traces of oxidization remain in the crevices and mouldings to give tone to the piece. When pewter has been kept in good condition, free from damp atmospheric conditions, and periodically polished, the high spots gain a smoothness and lustre which it is difficult to assimilate by artificial means, and it is this condition which seems to be preferred by the majority of serious collectors.

When pewter is found to possess only a dull grey smooth oxidization this may usually be removed by rubbing with a fine abrasive scouring powder and a damp rag. Avoid the coarse abrasives because the deep scratches which are left on the surface are difficult to eradicate and will prevent a high polish being obtained.

Occasionally some specimens will have a very hard black, or brownish, crust of oxide upon the whole surface, or this may, perhaps, have attacked odd patches of the area. In either event this is ugly, and should be removed, either wholly or partially according to the condition in which it is desired to keep the finished piece.

Hydrochloric Acid (more commonly known as Spirits of Salts) is the best medium for removal of this crust, and for normal purposes it should be diluted to about one part of acid to two parts water.

Great care must be taken whilst handling the acid, for its corrosive properties can do severe damage to hands and clothing, and also to the floor covering, if allowed to drip.

The safest method of use is for the hands to be covered with rubber gloves, and for the table or bench to be covered with several sheets of newspaper which can be changed frequently as they become splashed or saturated.

If the oxide patches are isolated they may be painted over liberally with acid—each small area being dealt with separately —and the acid left on to work for, perhaps, 15 or 20 minutes, as required. If the acid is then washed off and the patch rubbed with abrasive powder, or with emery cloth of very fine texture, the oxide will gradually come away. In severe cases it may be found expedient to use the acid undiluted, but do not leave it on for longer than necessary. It is better to make several assaults on the corrosion than to hope to clean off all the ugly marks with one application.

When the whole surface of an article is covered with hard scale it will probably be found beneficial to immerse it completely in a bath of acid, and here a diluted solution of one in three should be used, leaving the piece 'in soak' for an hour or so, testing occasionally to see whether the scale is ready to come away with gentle scouring.

When it is desired to leave the backs of plates, or the underside or inside of hollow articles, untouched these areas should be smeared with vaseline, and they will not be attacked by the acid.

Having taken off as much of the corrosion from an article as is desired the piece should then be thoroughly cleaned and washed by holding under a tap of running water, so that all traces of the acid are removed.

When pewter has been acid-cleaned the surface will, most probably, have lost its high polish, and this can be brought back only by hard rubbing and polishing. In the first instance it may be found helpful to use a fine wire-wool scourer, dipped in water so as not to cause more scratching to the surface than necessary and, as the surface improves, changing to fine scouring powder, and, lastly, finishing off by polishing with ordinary metal polish. Only hard work and continual polishing is now required to bring the article into first-class condition.

Dents and cracks which spoil the appearance of specimens can be treated by anyone handy with tools. Shallow dents in plates can be beaten out by placing the plate on a level surface, and by covering the dent with a piece of flat wood before hammering.

Where dents appear in the body of a hollow vessel, such as a flagon or tankard, it is usually possible to knock these up from the inside, using a heavy rounded object, such as the round knob of an iron poker. It is better to tap lightly and frequently than to use more drastic hammering.

When the dent appears on a plain cylindrical surface it will probably be found expedient to place a flat hard surface of wood or metal against the outside, and tap up the pewter against this from the inside, moving the plane surface round to follow the curve.

The repair of cracks and breaks on the surface of pewter is more of an expert task, but if one is familiar with ordinary soft soldering procedure, a satisfactory repair can be effected with care.

The solder to be used in such cases should have a melting point slightly below that of the pewter to be repaired, otherwise disaster will follow. It is a good thing to have a piece of Britannia metal, such as a fragment from an old teapot, available to use as a solder.

This melts rather more quickly than true pewter, but will not be very different in colour when used sparingly on the repair.

Ordinary lead solder, or plumber's metal, is of a much greyer colour, and repairs done with it will always be apparent, particularly when the article needs re-cleaning.

The surfaces to be joined should be well cleaned by scraping or filing, and the repair, where possible, should be done from the inside, or underside. It may be found helpful to leave a slight 'V' depression into which the solder should be run. The edges of the job should be treated with a 'flux', and the soldering iron needs to be of ample weight to hold the heat for a sufficient length of time.

It is not proposed to go into a detailed description of soldering. It is far better for the beginner to practise soldering on some insignificant object before attempting a major job on some more important piece. There is always the risk that, by inexperience, the solderer will melt away a section of the article he is working upon. It will be found far more difficult to patch the job afterwards and so, when difficulty is expected, it is better to take the work to an experienced professional repairer than to risk irreparable damage.

When a satisfactory repair has been effected, and the surplus metal carefully filed away, it will be necessary to re-surface the area of the repair. This can be done by trimming with abrasives, gradually reducing the coarseness, until the finishing-off stage with metal polish.

The repaired area is now most likely to be much brighter and highly polished than the rest of the piece, and it may be darkened, if necessary, by the application of a little diluted nitric acid.

After the correct tone has been obtained the area should be well washed, and the whole piece cleaned to the desired condition.

BIBLIOGRAPHY

COTTERELL HOWARD H.: 'Old Pewter, and how to collect it', *Collector's Lists,* March, 1913.

—— 'Old Pewter or Britannia Metal', *Connoisseur*, March, 1921.

—— 'Old Pewter, and its Story', *The Queen*, 22nd July, 29th July, 5th August, and 19th August, 1931.

——'Pewter Collectors and their Motives', *Antique Collector*, 21st November, 1931.

—— 'Nature's Gilding on Old Pewter Vessels', *Apollo*, September, 1933.

SUTHERLAND GRAEME, A. V.: 'The Society of Pewter Collectors', *Connoisseur*, December, 1933.

BIBLIOGRAPHY

Below is given a list of the more useful books which deal specifically with British pewterware and pewterers. Most of these cover the subject generally, but at the foot of each chapter will be found a list of articles from magazines and periodicals, written from a more specialized angle, and relating particularly to the matter dealt with in the respective chapters.

BELL, MALCOLM: *Old Pewter*, George Newnes, London, and Charles Scribner's Sons, New York, 1905. Rev. ed., London, 1913.

BURNS, REV. THOMAS: *Old Scottish Communion Plate*, Clark, Edinburgh, 1892.

COTTERELL, HOWARD H.: *Old Pewter, its Makers and Marks*, Batsford, London, 1929.

—— 'National Types of Old Pewter', *Antiques*, Boston, Mass., 1925.

DE NAVARRO, ANTONIO: 'Causeries on English Pewter', *Country Life*, London, and Scribner's, New York, 1911.

INGLEBY WOOD, LINDSAY: *Scottish Pewterware and Pewterers*, G. A. Morton, Edinburgh, 1907.

MASSÉ, H. J. L. J.: *Pewter Plate*, Bell, London, 1904. 2nd ed. (revised), 1911.

——*Chats on Old Pewter* (revised by R. F. Michaelis; new section on American pewter by H. J. Kauffman), Dover, New York, 1971. (Earlier editions by Benn, London, 1911 and 1949.)

——*The Pewter Collector* (revised by R. F. Michaelis), Barrie & Jenkins, London, 1971. (Earlier edition by Herbert Jenkins, London, 1921).

MICHAELIS, RONALD F.: *British Pewter*, Ward Lock, London, 1969.

PEWTERERS' COMPANY, THE WORSHIPFUL: *Short History, and Catalogue of Its Pewterware*, compiled for the Company by R. F. Michaelis, and privately printed in London, 1968.

PRICE, F. G. HILTON: *Old Base Metal Spoons*, Batsford, London, 1908.

WELCH, CHARLES: *History of the Worshipful Company of Pewterers, of London*, Blades, East & Blades, London, 1902.

INDEX

PLATES

PLATE I

FIG. 16. Narrow-bordered deep dish, with centre boss, of the type known as 'Spanish trencher', diameter 13 inches. (Early to mid-17th century.)

FIG. 17. Pair of small 'saucers', diameter 6 inches, with rim 1⅛ inches wide. On the front of the rim is stamped a Crowned Tudor Rose, and the initials 'E' and 'R'. Maker's mark on reverse. c.1570. From Hampton Court Palace. (Photograph reproduced by gracious permission of Her Majesty the Queen.)

PLATE II

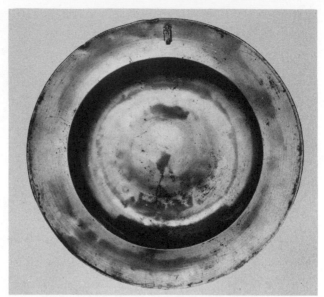

FIG. 18. Shallow bowl plate, dug up at Guy's Hospital, London, in 1899. Stamped on the rim with a Crowned Feather. Maker's mark on reverse. Probably early 16th century. (From the collection of the late Mr. R. W. Cooper.)

FIG. 19. Shallow bowl plate, with centre boss; stamped on the rim with a 'Spur prong and rowel', and the ownership initials (as drawn). Of coeval date with the plate shown in Fig. 18. No maker's mark. Diameter $10\frac{1}{8}$ inches, rim width $1\frac{1}{16}$ inches.

PLATE III

Fig. 20. Broad-rimmed paten, diameter 9⅜ inches, rim width
2 inches. Mid-17th century. (From the collection of Mr. C. C.
Minchin.)

Fig. 21. Dish of the type known as 'Cardinal's Hat', with deep well and
centre boss. Diameter 15 inches. c.1650–75. Shown with a pair of
Stuart period candlesticks, and a salt, of c.1700.

PLATE IV

FIG. 22.   Narrow-bordered plate, diameter $9\frac{1}{2}$ inches; and a similar
dish, diameter $15\frac{3}{4}$ inches. $c.1670$–90.

FIG. 23.   Three five-lobed, or 'wavy-edge', plates of $c.1750$–75.

PLATE V

FIG. 24. A two-handled Posset Cup, engraved in 'wriggled-work' with portraits of William III and Mary. c.1690. (Shown by permission of the Committee of the Guildhall Library and Museum, London.)

FIG. 25. A group of late beaker-type measures, or drinking cups, of ½-pint capacity. Dating from c.1780 to c.1840.

Fig. 26. A 'tulip-shaped' tankard, with domed cover and 'chairback' thumbpiece. Made by William Eden (or Eddon), London, c.1730.

Fig. 27. A group of Stuart tankards, showing a variety of ornamental thumbpieces, c.1680–90.

PLATE VII

Fig. 28. Two domed-top tankards, with 'ball' terminal to handle, *c.*1700–10; and a flagon, of *c.*1750. (From the collection of the late Mr. E. Richmond Paton.)

Fig. 29. Three domed-top tankards, with 'fish-tail' terminal to handle. The first item is of 1½ pint, and the third of 1 pint capacity, *c.*1710–20. The central tankard is of ½ gallon capacity, *c.*1775.

PLATE VIII

FIG. 30. Two early lidless tankards; the first of early Queen Anne period, and the second, with hooped bands, of c.1680.

FIG. 31. Two early lidless tankards, of tapering form; that on the left with an inscription reading 'Andr Gladman att ye George Inn, Layton buzard', c.1695–1705. Height 5½ inches to lip. (*Right*) a slightly later example, height 6⅞ inches. c.1710–15.

PLATE IX

FIG. 32. Three late Georgian tankards, or measures, of pint and quart capacities. Late 18th or early 19th century.

FIG. 33. A group of early Victorian tavern pots, used as both tankard and measure. (*From left to right*) the first is a Norfolk and Suffolk type; the second type is also found with single-curved handle; the two items (Nos. 3 and 4) are part of a set of four, comprising quart, pint, $\frac{1}{2}$ pint and $\frac{1}{4}$ pint; these are sometimes found with domed covers. The last item is of similar form, but with a lip, and is, therefore, more likely to be a measure.

FIG. 35. Baluster measure, with 'ball and wedge' thumbpiece, of 1 pint capacity (Old English Wine Standard), c. 1650–75. (By courtesy of the Directors of the Victoria and Albert Museum, London.)

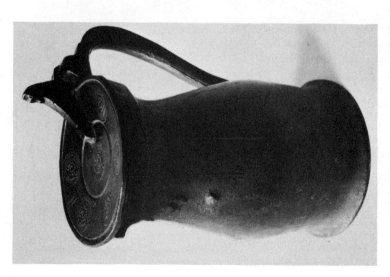

FIG. 34. A baluster wine measure, with cast ornament at top of the 'wedge' thumbpiece, c. 1650–70. (Guildhall Museum, London.)

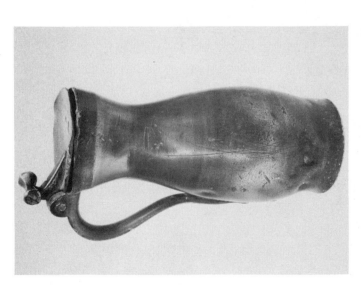

PLATE XI

Fig. 37. A baluster measure, with 'bud and wedge' thumbpiece, made by Nicholas Marriott, London, c.1690–1700. (The six marks apparent on the cover are not maker's marks, but are 'housemarks' of a former owner.) (From collection of the late Mr. R. W. Cooper.)

Fig. 36. Baluster measure of quart capacity, with 'hammerhead' thumbpiece. Late sixteenth century. (Richard Mundey collection.)

PLATE XII

FIG. 40. Scottish baluster measure, with 'embryo-shell' thumbpiece, c.1800.

FIG. 39. A Scottish baluster measure, with 'ball and bar' thumbpiece, c.1790.

FIG. 38. Baluster measure, with 'double volute' thumbpiece, of quart capacity, made by William Fasson, London, c.1760.

PLATE XIII

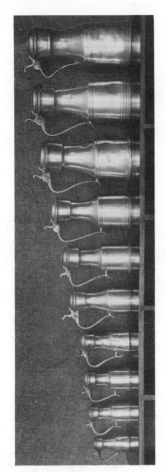

FIG. 41. A fine range of Scottish tappit hen measures, ranging from the ½ gallon (Imperial) to the Scots gill. *c.*1750–1830. (From the collection of the late Mr. Lewis Clapperton.)

FIG. 42. Group of Scottish tappit hen measures showing, respectively, the plain cover (as above), *c.*1790; the 'crested' cover (made in three sizes only), *c.*1800–30; and the lidless form (made in Imperial sizes), *c.*1830.

PLATE XIV

FIG. 43. Channel Islands measures, 'Guernsey' type, with bands of decoration round the neck and drum, and a moulded foot flange.

FIG. 44. Channel Islands measures, 'Jersey' type.

PLATE XV

FIG. 47. A 'ball knopped' candlestick, with gadrooned moulding and octagonal base, c.1675. (From the Cooper collection.)

FIG. 46. An early 'low bell' based candlestick, 7½ inches high. First half of the 17th century. (From the Clapperton collection.)

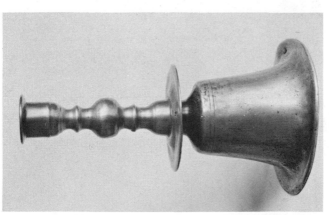

FIG. 45. A candlestick with 'high bell' base, 8 inches high. First half of the 17th century. (Originally in the de Navarro collection, but whereabouts now unknown.)

PLATE XVI

Fig. 48. Various 17th-century candlesticks and tapersticks. (From the collection of Mr. C. C. Minchin.)

PLATE XVII

FIG. 49. Three salts; the first and third of 'Capstan' type, c.1685; and (*in the centre*) an elongated octagonal salt, of c.1715. In the background is a 'saucer', probably 16th century. (From the Cooper collection.)

FIG. 50. Two 'capstan' salts, of c.1685. (From the Clapperton collection.)

PLATE XVIII

FIG. 51. Hanging rack, displaying spoons with cast royal portraits, ranging over the reigns of William III and Mary, Queen Anne and George III and Charlotte.

PLATE XIX

FIG. 52. Various early spoons, and an elongated salt, shown on an attractive oak spoon rack. (From the Cooper collection.)

PLATE XX

FIG. 53. Straight-sided porringer, with 'double dolphin' ear, c.1670.

FIG. 54. 'Booged' porringer, with 'double dolphin' ear, c.1685.

FIG. 55. 'Coronet' handled porringer, with flat base, c.1720.

PLATE XXI

FIG. 56. Blood porringer, or bleeding bowl, with gradation marks in the bowl, made by 'W. & S.', Salisbury. (Early 19th century.) (By kind permission of the Salisbury, South Wilts. and Blackmore Museum.)

FIG. 57. A caudle cup, height 4⅛ inches; diameter at top 4½ inches. c.1720.

PLATE XXII

FIG. 58. A wassail bowl, with two curved handles, height 6¾ inches; width at top 6½ inches, c.1675.

FIG. 59. A loving cup, height 5½ inches; width across handles 7¾ inches; made by Robert Bush and . . . Walter, Bristol, c.1775.

PLATE XXIII

Fig. 60. Elizabethan flagon, 12¼ inches high overall.
(Originally in the Minchin collection, now owned by
the Worshipful Company of Pewterers. When illustrated
in the 1955 edition this flagon was in unrepaired state, but
is now shown reconditioned.)

PLATE XXIV

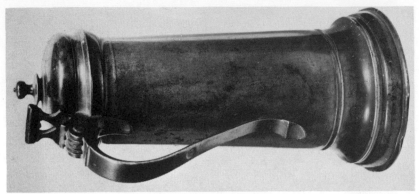

Fig. 61, (*left*). Flagon with knopped 'bun', cover, height to top of thumbpiece, 11 inches, c.1605–15.

Fig. 62, (*right*) Flagon with knopped 'muffin', cover and 'heart-pierced' thumbpiece, c.1630. (From the collection of the late Mr. E. W. Turner.)

PLATE XXV

Fig. 63. Two flagons with 'beefeater' cover and spreading base, (*a*) at left, with dated touch, 'R.B.' and Anchor, *c.*1670, from the Minchin collection; and (*b*) with mark of 'R.B.' and 'fleur de lys', formerly in the collection of the late Dr. R. Blake Marsh, now bequeathed to the Worshipful Company of Pewterers.

Fig. 64. Two flagons, with 'broken' handle and 'chairback' thumbpiece; that on the left dated 1743; and that on the right dated 1730.

PLATE XXVI

Fig. 65.   A fine range of English pewter flagons, of all periods from c.1610 to c.1730.
(See pages 71-2 for descriptions.)   (From the collection of Mr. C. C. Minchin.)

PLATE XXVII

FIG. 66. Irish fla-
gon, with domed
cover and spread-
ing base, *c.*1775.

FIG. 67. Two fla-
gons, of Scottish
type, made by
Richard Going,
Bristol, *c.*1750;
and a triple-reeded
dish, with broad
rim, made by
John Cave
(senior), Bristol,
*c.*1690.

PLATE XXVIII

FIG. 68. A tazza, or footed plate, 7⅛ inches diameter at top, made by John Shorey, Senior, London, c.1685–90.

FIG. 69. Alms dish, with single-reeded rim (one of a pair), 13½ inches diameter, with both punched and hammered decoration, made by Samuel Smith, London, c.1730.

PLATE XXIX

Fig. 70. A collection of Scottish pewter-mounted snuff mulls. Early 19th century.

Fig. 71. A group of pounce pots and pepper pots, of the late 18th and early 19th centuries.

PLATE XXX

FIG. 72A. Pewter inkstand, 'The Guifte of Mr. Martin Bonnde',
with the cover closed, showing the inscription and date.
FIG. 72B. The same inkstand, with the hinged cover open. (In
the possession of the Governors of St. Bartholomew's Hospital.
London.)

PLATE XXXI

FIG. 73. A pair of 19th-century fireside ornaments in pewter, set on japanned iron bases. Height overall 10½ inches.

FIG. 74. 'Billy & Charley' faked mediæval vases and figurines of ecclesiastics.

PLATE XXXII

FIG. 75. A fine Stuart flat-topped tankard, decorated in 'wriggled-work', made by Peter Duffield, London, c.1670. Height 4 inches to lip. (From the collection of Mr. C. C. Minchin.)

FIG. 76. A narrow-rimmed plate, 8½ inches diameter, decorated in 'wriggled-work', c.1680-90.

PLATE XXXIII

FIG. 77. A superb Charles II broad-rimmed dish, with Stuart Arms and border decoration in 'wriggled-work', dated 1662. (Collection of the late Mr. R. W. Cooper.)

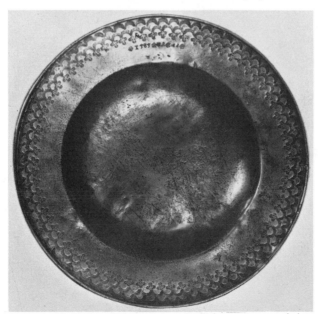

FIG. 78. Elizabethan dish, with 'punched' decoration round the border, incorporating the date 1585. (Formerly in the collection of the late Mr. F. Jaeger, now owned by the Worshipful Company of Pewterers.)

PLATE XXXIV

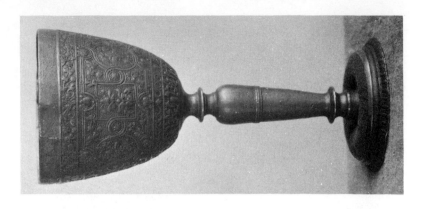

Fig. 79. The 'William Grainger' candlestick, with relief-cast decoration, dated 1616. Height 9½ inches. (By courtesy of the Victoria and Albert Museum, London.)

Fig. 80. Footed cup, or chalice, decorated in cast relief, with arabesque designs. Probably Elizabethan. (By courtesy of the Victoria and Albert Museum.)

PLATE XXXV

FIG. 81A. A tazza, or footed plate, with cast ornamentation, dated 1616, and with later inscription dated 1621, at the Church of St. Mary's, West Shefford, Berks.

FIG. 81B. Showing the ornamented foot and stem of the tazza in Fig. 81A.

(Photographs by kind permission of Mr. C. C. Minchin, Reading.)

PLATE XXXVI

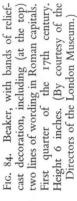

FIG. 84. Beaker, with bands of relief-cast decoration, including (at the top) two lines of wording in Roman capitals. First quarter of the 17th century. Height 6 inches. (By courtesy of the Directors of the London Museum.)

FIG. 83. Beaker, with bands of relief-cast decoration, incorporating the Prince of Wales's feathers, the Tudor Rose, and the Royal Stuart Arms. 4⅝ inches high. Early 17th century. (From the collection of the late Mr. A. B. Yeates, now at the Victoria and Albert Museum.)

FIG. 82. Beaker of Henry, son of James I, bearing the Prince of Wales's feathers, with initials 'H' and 'P' (Henricus Princeps), c.1610–12. Height 6 inches. (In the author's collection.)

PLATE XXXVII

FIG. 86. Relief-cast plate, or flagon stand, 5 inches diameter, showing bands of running ornamentation of somewhat similar character to the foregoing pieces. Dug up in London. Probably Elizabethan. (By courtesy of the Directors of the London Museum.)

FIG. 85. Early Stuart beaker, with all-over relief-cast decoration, incorporating the Stuart Arms, and the Rose and Crown. In the smaller cartouches, below the raised flange, are representations of the Thistle, the Rose, and the fleur de lys. 4½ inches high. (By courtesy of the Victoria and Albert Museum.)

PLATE XXXVIII

FIG. 87. Wine taster, with ear in cast relief, and with a Tudor Rose design cast in the base. Diameter of bowl $2\frac{7}{8}$ inches. Early to mid-17th century. (In the author's collection.)

FIG. 88. Two-eared commemorative porringer, with relief-cast bust of William of Orange in the centre of bowl. c.1690–1700. (In the author's collection.)

PLATE XXXIX

FIG. 89. Spoons with royal portraits cast on the handles. From left to right, (i) and (ii) William and Mary; (iii) Queen Anne; and (iv) George III and Charlotte. (Collection of the late Capt. A. V. Sutherland Graeme.)

PLATE XL

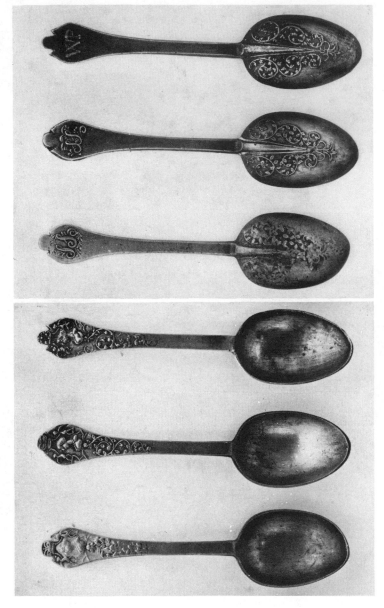

Fig. 90. Three spoons, each with a relief-cast portrait of Queen Anne at top, and (in the same order) the reverses, showing relief-cast initials at top and decoration on the bowls, c.1702. (In the author's collection.)

A CATALOGUE OF SELECTED DOVER BOOKS
IN ALL FIELDS OF INTEREST

A CATALOGUE OF SELECTED DOVER BOOKS
IN ALL FIELDS OF INTEREST

AMERICA'S OLD MASTERS, James T. Flexner. Four men emerged unexpectedly from provincial 18th century America to leadership in European art: Benjamin West, J. S. Copley, C. R. Peale, Gilbert Stuart. Brilliant coverage of lives and contributions. Revised, 1967 edition. 69 plates. 365pp. of text.
21806-6 Paperbound $3.00

FIRST FLOWERS OF OUR WILDERNESS: AMERICAN PAINTING, THE COLONIAL PERIOD, James T. Flexner. Painters, and regional painting traditions from earliest Colonial times up to the emergence of Copley, West and Peale Sr., Foster, Gustavus Hesselius, Feke, John Smibert and many anonymous painters in the primitive manner. Engaging presentation, with 162 illustrations. xxii + 368pp.
22180-6 Paperbound $3.50

THE LIGHT OF DISTANT SKIES: AMERICAN PAINTING, 1760-1835, James T. Flexner. The great generation of early American painters goes to Europe to learn and to teach: West, Copley, Gilbert Stuart and others. Allston, Trumbull, Morse; also contemporary American painters—primitives, derivatives, academics—who remained in America. 102 illustrations. xiii + 306pp.
22179-2 Paperbound $3.00

A HISTORY OF THE RISE AND PROGRESS OF THE ARTS OF DESIGN IN THE UNITED STATES, William Dunlap. Much the richest mine of information on early American painters, sculptors, architects, engravers, miniaturists, etc. The only source of information for scores of artists, the major primary source for many others. Unabridged reprint of rare original 1834 edition, with new introduction by James T. Flexner, and 394 new illustrations. 6⅝ x 9⅝.
21695-0, 21696-9, 21697-7 Three volumes, Paperbound $13.50

EPOCHS OF CHINESE AND JAPANESE ART, Ernest F. Fenollosa. From primitive Chinese art to the 20th century, thorough history, explanation of every important art period and form, including Japanese woodcuts; main stress on China and Japan, but Tibet, Korea also included. Still unexcelled for its detailed, rich coverage of cultural background, aesthetic elements, diffusion studies, particularly of the historical period. 2nd, 1913 edition. 242 illustrations. lii + 439pp. of text.
20364-6, 20365-4 Two volumes, Paperbound $6.00

THE GENTLE ART OF MAKING ENEMIES, James A. M. Whistler. Greatest wit of his day deflates Oscar Wilde, Ruskin, Swinburne; strikes back at inane critics, exhibitions, art journalism; aesthetics of impressionist revolution in most striking form. Highly readable classic by great painter. Reproduction of edition designed by Whistler. Introduction by Alfred Werner. xxxvi + 334pp.
21875-9 Paperbound $2.50

ALPHABETS AND ORNAMENTS, Ernst Lehner. Well-known pictorial source for decorative alphabets, script examples, cartouches, frames, decorative title pages, calligraphic initials, borders, similar material. 14th to 19th century, mostly European. Useful in almost any graphic arts designing, varied styles. 750 illustrations. 256pp. 7 x 10.   21905-4 Paperbound $4.00

PAINTING: A CREATIVE APPROACH, Norman Colquhoun. For the beginner simple guide provides an instructive approach to painting: major stumbling blocks for beginner; overcoming them, technical points; paints and pigments; oil painting; watercolor and other media and color. New section on "plastic" paints. Glossary. Formerly *Paint Your Own Pictures*. 221pp.   22000-1 Paperbound $1.75

THE ENJOYMENT AND USE OF COLOR, Walter Sargent. Explanation of the relations between colors themselves and between colors in nature and art, including hundreds of little-known facts about color values, intensities, effects of high and low illumination, complementary colors. Many practical hints for painters, references to great masters. 7 color plates, 29 illustrations. x + 274pp.
20944-X Paperbound $2.50

THE NOTEBOOKS OF LEONARDO DA VINCI, compiled and edited by Jean Paul Richter. 1566 extracts from original manuscripts reveal the full range of Leonardo's versatile genius: all his writings on painting, sculpture, architecture, anatomy, astronomy, geography, topography, physiology, mining, music, etc., in both Italian and English, with 186 plates of manuscript pages and more than 500 additional drawings. Includes studies for the Last Supper, the lost Sforza monument, and other works. Total of xlvii + 866pp. 7⅞ x 10¾.
22572-0, 22573-9 Two volumes, Paperbound $10.00

MONTGOMERY WARD CATALOGUE OF 1895. Tea gowns, yards of flannel and pillow-case lace, stereoscopes, books of gospel hymns, the New Improved Singer Sewing Machine, side saddles, milk skimmers, straight-edged razors, high-button shoes, spittoons, and on and on . . . listing some 25,000 items, practically all illustrated. Essential to the shoppers of the 1890's, it is our truest record of the spirit of the period. Unaltered reprint of Issue No. 57, Spring and Summer 1895. Introduction by Boris Emmet. Innumerable illustrations. xiii + 624pp. 8½ x 11⅝.
22377-9 Paperbound $6.95

THE CRYSTAL PALACE EXHIBITION ILLUSTRATED CATALOGUE (LONDON, 1851). One of the wonders of the modern world—the Crystal Palace Exhibition in which all the nations of the civilized world exhibited their achievements in the arts and sciences—presented in an equally important illustrated catalogue. More than 1700 items pictured with accompanying text—ceramics, textiles, cast-iron work, carpets, pianos, sleds, razors, wall-papers, billiard tables, beehives, silverware and hundreds of other artifacts—represent the focal point of Victorian culture in the Western World. Probably the largest collection of Victorian decorative art ever assembled—indispensable for antiquarians and designers. Unabridged republication of the Art-Journal Catalogue of the Great Exhibition of 1851, with all terminal essays. New introduction by John Gloag, F.S.A. xxxiv + 426pp. 9 x 12.
22503-8 Paperbound $4.50

A HISTORY OF COSTUME, Carl Köhler. Definitive history, based on surviving pieces of clothing primarily, and paintings, statues, etc. secondarily. Highly readable text, supplemented by 594 illustrations of costumes of the ancient Mediterranean peoples, Greece and Rome, the Teutonic prehistoric period; costumes of the Middle Ages, Renaissance, Baroque, 18th and 19th centuries. Clear, measured patterns are provided for many clothing articles. Approach is practical throughout. Enlarged by Emma von Sichart. 464pp.   21030-8 Paperbound $3.00

ORIENTAL RUGS, ANTIQUE AND MODERN, Walter A. Hawley. A complete and authoritative treatise on the Oriental rug—where they are made, by whom and how, designs and symbols, characteristics in detail of the six major groups, how to distinguish them and how to buy them. Detailed technical data is provided on periods, weaves, warps, wefts, textures, sides, ends and knots, although no technical background is required for an understanding. 11 color plates, 80 halftones, 4 maps. vi + 320pp. 6⅛ x 9⅛.   22366-3 Paperbound $5.00

TEN BOOKS ON ARCHITECTURE, Vitruvius. By any standards the most important book on architecture ever written. Early Roman discussion of aesthetics of building, construction methods, orders, sites, and every other aspect of architecture has inspired, instructed architecture for about 2,000 years. Stands behind Palladio, Michelangelo, Bramante, Wren, countless others. Definitive Morris H. Morgan translation. 68 illustrations. xii + 331pp.   20645-9 Paperbound $2.50

THE FOUR BOOKS OF ARCHITECTURE, Andrea Palladio. Translated into every major Western European language in the two centuries following its publication in 1570, this has been one of the most influential books in the history of architecture. Complete reprint of the 1738 Isaac Ware edition. New introduction by Adolf Placzek, Columbia Univ. 216 plates. xxii + 110pp. of text. 9½ x 12¾.
21308-0 Clothbound $10.00

STICKS AND STONES: A STUDY OF AMERICAN ARCHITECTURE AND CIVILIZATION, Lewis Mumford.One of the great classics of American cultural history. American architecture from the medieval-inspired earliest forms to the early 20th century; evolution of structure and style, and reciprocal influences on environment. 21 photographic illustrations. 238pp.   20202-X Paperbound $2.00

THE AMERICAN BUILDER'S COMPANION, Asher Benjamin. The most widely used early 19th century architectural style and source book, for colonial up into Greek Revival periods. Extensive development of geometry of carpentering, construction of sashes, frames, doors, stairs; plans and elevations of domestic and other buildings. Hundreds of thousands of houses were built according to this book, now invaluable to historians, architects, restorers, etc. 1827 edition. 59 plates. 114pp. 7⅞ x 10¾.
22236-5 Paperbound $3.00

DUTCH HOUSES IN THE HUDSON VALLEY BEFORE 1776, Helen Wilkinson Reynolds. The standard survey of the Dutch colonial house and outbuildings, with constructional features, decoration, and local history associated with individual homesteads. Introduction by Franklin D. Roosevelt. Map. 150 illustrations. 469pp. 6⅝ x 9¼.   21469-9 Paperbound $3.50

THE ARCHITECTURE OF COUNTRY HOUSES, Andrew J. Downing. Together with Vaux's *Villas and Cottages* this is the basic book for Hudson River Gothic architecture of the middle Victorian period. Full, sound discussions of general aspects of housing, architecture, style, decoration, furnishing, together with scores of detailed house plans, illustrations of specific buildings, accompanied by full text. Perhaps the most influential single American architectural book. 1850 edition. Introduction by J. Stewart Johnson. 321 figures, 34 architectural designs. xvi + 560pp.
22003-6 Paperbound $4.00

LOST EXAMPLES OF COLONIAL ARCHITECTURE, John Mead Howells. Full-page photographs of buildings that have disappeared or been so altered as to be denatured, including many designed by major early American architects. 245 plates. xvii + 248pp. 7⅞ x 10¾.
21143-6 Paperbound $3.00

DOMESTIC ARCHITECTURE OF THE AMERICAN COLONIES AND OF THE EARLY REPUBLIC, Fiske Kimball. Foremost architect and restorer of Williamsburg and Monticello covers nearly 200 homes between 1620-1825. Architectural details, construction, style features, special fixtures, floor plans, etc. Generally considered finest work in its area. 219 illustrations of houses, doorways, windows, capital mantels. xx + 314pp. 7⅞ x 10¾.
21743-4 Paperbound $3.50

EARLY AMERICAN ROOMS: 1650-1858, edited by Russell Hawes Kettell. Tour of 12 rooms, each representative of a different era in American history and each furnished, decorated, designed and occupied in the style of the era. 72 plans and elevations, 8-page color section, etc., show fabrics, wall papers, arrangements, etc. Full descriptive text. xvii + 200pp. of text. 8⅜ x 11¼.
21633-0 Paperbound $5.00

THE FITZWILLIAM VIRGINAL BOOK, edited by J. Fuller Maitland and W. B. Squire. Full modern printing of famous early 17th-century ms. volume of 300 works by Morley, Byrd, Bull, Gibbons, etc. For piano or other modern keyboard instrument; easy to read format. xxxvi + 938pp. 8⅜ x 11.
21068-5, 21069-3 Two volumes, Paperbound $8.00

HARPSICHORD MUSIC, Johann Sebastian Bach. Bach Gesellschaft edition. A rich selection of Bach's masterpieces for the harpsichord: the six English Suites, six French Suites, the six Partitas (Clavierübung part I), the Goldberg Variations (Clavierübung part IV), the fifteen Two-Part Inventions and the fifteen Three-Part Sinfonias. Clearly reproduced on large sheets with ample margins; eminently playable. vi + 312pp. 8⅛ x 11.
22360-4 Paperbound $5.00

THE MUSIC OF BACH: AN INTRODUCTION, Charles Sanford Terry. A fine, nontechnical introduction to Bach's music, both instrumental and vocal. Covers organ music, chamber music, passion music, other types. Analyzes themes, developments, innovations. x + 114pp.
21075-8 Paperbound $1.25

BEETHOVEN AND HIS NINE SYMPHONIES, Sir George Grove. Noted British musicologist provides best history, analysis, commentary on symphonies. Very thorough, rigorously accurate; necessary to both advanced student and amateur music lover. 436 musical passages. vii + 407 pp.
20334-4 Paperbound $2.25

JOHANN SEBASTIAN BACH, Philipp Spitta. One of the great classics of musicology, this definitive analysis of Bach's music (and life) has never been surpassed. Lucid, nontechnical analyses of hundreds of pieces (30 pages devoted to St. Matthew Passion, 26 to B Minor Mass). Also includes major analysis of 18th-century music. 450 musical examples. 40-page musical supplement. Total of xx + 1799pp.
(EUK) 22278-0, 22279-9 Two volumes, Clothbound $15.00

MOZART AND HIS PIANO CONCERTOS, Cuthbert Girdlestone. The only full-length study of an important area of Mozart's creativity. Provides detailed analyses of all 23 concertos, traces inspirational sources. 417 musical examples. Second edition. 509pp. (USO) 21271-8 Paperbound $3.50

THE PERFECT WAGNERITE: A COMMENTARY ON THE NIBLUNG'S RING, George Bernard Shaw. Brilliant and still relevant criticism in remarkable essays on Wagner's Ring cycle, Shaw's ideas on political and social ideology behind the plots, role of Leitmotifs, vocal requisites, etc. Prefaces. xxi + 136pp.
21707-8 Paperbound $1.50

DON GIOVANNI, W. A. Mozart. Complete libretto, modern English translation; biographies of composer and librettist; accounts of early performances and critical reaction. Lavishly illustrated. All the material you need to understand and appreciate this great work. Dover Opera Guide and Libretto Series; translated and introduced by Ellen Bleiler. 92 illustrations. 209pp.
21134-7 Paperbound $1.50

HIGH FIDELITY SYSTEMS: A LAYMAN'S GUIDE, Roy F. Allison. All the basic information you need for setting up your own audio system: high fidelity and stereo record players, tape records, F.M. Connections, adjusting tone arm, cartridge, checking needle alignment, positioning speakers, phasing speakers, adjusting hums, trouble-shooting, maintenance, and similar topics. Enlarged 1965 edition. More than 50 charts, diagrams, photos. iv + 91pp. 21514-8 Paperbound $1.25

REPRODUCTION OF SOUND, Edgar Villchur. Thorough coverage for laymen of high fidelity systems, reproducing systems in general, needles, amplifiers, preamps, loudspeakers, feedback, explaining physical background. "A rare talent for making technicalities vividly comprehensible," R. Darrell, High Fidelity. 69 figures. iv + 92pp. 21515-6 Paperbound $1.00

HEAR ME TALKIN' TO YA: THE STORY OF JAZZ AS TOLD BY THE MEN WHO MADE IT, Nat Shapiro and Nat Hentoff. Louis Armstrong, Fats Waller, Jo Jones, Clarence Williams, Billy Holiday, Duke Ellington, Jelly Roll Morton and dozens of other jazz greats tell how it was in Chicago's South Side, New Orleans, depression Harlem and the modern West Coast as jazz was born and grew. xvi + 429pp.
21726-4 Paperbound $2.50

FABLES OF AESOP, translated by Sir Roger L'Estrange. A reproduction of the very rare 1931 Paris edition; a selection of the most interesting fables, together with 50 imaginative drawings by Alexander Calder. v + 128pp. 6½x9¼.
21780-9 Paperbound $1.25

POEMS OF ANNE BRADSTREET, edited with an introduction by Robert Hutchinson. A new selection of poems by America's first poet and perhaps the first significant woman poet in the English language. 48 poems display her development in works of considerable variety—love poems, domestic poems, religious meditations, formal elegies, "quaternions," etc. Notes, bibliography. viii + 222pp.
22160-1 Paperbound $2.00

THREE GOTHIC NOVELS: THE CASTLE OF OTRANTO BY HORACE WALPOLE; VATHEK BY WILLIAM BECKFORD; THE VAMPYRE BY JOHN POLIDORI, WITH FRAGMENT OF A NOVEL BY LORD BYRON, edited by E. F. Bleiler. The first Gothic novel, by Walpole; the finest Oriental tale in English, by Beckford; powerful Romantic supernatural story in versions by Polidori and Byron. All extremely important in history of literature; all still exciting, packed with supernatural thrills, ghosts, haunted castles, magic, etc. xl + 291pp.
21232-7 Paperbound $2.00

THE BEST TALES OF HOFFMANN, E. T. A. Hoffmann. 10 of Hoffmann's most important stories, in modern re-editings of standard translations: Nutcracker and the King of Mice, Signor Formica, Automata, The Sandman, Rath Krespel, The Golden Flowerpot, Master Martin the Cooper, The Mines of Falun, The King's Betrothed, A New Year's Eve Adventure. 7 illustrations by Hoffmann. Edited by E. F. Bleiler. xxxix + 419pp.
21793-0 Paperbound $2.50

GHOST AND HORROR STORIES OF AMBROSE BIERCE, Ambrose Bierce. 23 strikingly modern stories of the horrors latent in the human mind: The Eyes of the Panther, The Damned Thing, An Occurrence at Owl Creek Bridge, An Inhabitant of Carcosa, etc., plus the dream-essay, Visions of the Night. Edited by E. F. Bleiler. xxii + 199pp.
20767-6 Paperbound $1.50

BEST GHOST STORIES OF J. S. LeFANU, J. Sheridan LeFanu. Finest stories by Victorian master often considered greatest supernatural writer of all. Carmilla, Green Tea, The Haunted Baronet, The Familiar, and 12 others. Most never before available in the U. S. A. Edited by E. F. Bleiler. 8 illustrations from Victorian publications. xvii + 467pp.
20415-4 Paperbound $2.50

THE TIME STREAM, THE GREATEST ADVENTURE, AND THE PURPLE SAPPHIRE— THREE SCIENCE FICTION NOVELS, John Taine (Eric Temple Bell). Great American mathematician was also foremost science fiction novelist of the 1920's. *The Time Stream,* one of all-time classics, uses concepts of circular time; *The Greatest Adventure,* incredibly ancient biological experiments from Antarctica threaten to escape; The *Purple Sapphire,* superscience, lost races in Central Tibet, survivors of the Great Race. 4 illustrations by Frank R. Paul. v + 532pp.
21180-0 Paperbound $3.00

SEVEN SCIENCE FICTION NOVELS, H. G. Wells. The standard collection of the great novels. Complete, unabridged. *First Men in the Moon, Island of Dr. Moreau, War of the Worlds, Food of the Gods, Invisible Man, Time Machine, In the Days of the Comet.* Not only science fiction fans, but every educated person owes it to himself to read these novels. 1015pp.
20264-X Clothbound $5.00

LAST AND FIRST MEN AND STAR MAKER, TWO SCIENCE FICTION NOVELS, Olaf Stapledon. Greatest future histories in science fiction. In the first, human intelligence is the "hero," through strange paths of evolution, interplanetary invasions, incredible technologies, near extinctions and reemergences. Star Maker describes the quest of a band of star rovers for intelligence itself, through time and space: weird inhuman civilizations, crustacean minds, symbiotic worlds, etc. Complete, unabridged. v + 438pp. 21962-3 Paperbound $2.00

THREE PROPHETIC NOVELS, H. G. WELLS. Stages of a consistently planned future for mankind. *When the Sleeper Wakes,* and *A Story of the Days to Come,* anticipate *Brave New World* and *1984,* in the 21st Century; *The Time Machine,* only complete version in print, shows farther future and the end of mankind. All show Wells's greatest gifts as storyteller and novelist. Edited by E. F. Bleiler. x + 335pp. (USO) 20605-X Paperbound $2.00

THE DEVIL'S DICTIONARY, Ambrose Bierce. America's own Oscar Wilde—Ambrose Bierce—offers his barbed iconoclastic wisdom in over 1,000 definitions hailed by H. L. Mencken as "some of the most gorgeous witticisms in the English language." 145pp. 20487-1 Paperbound $1.25

MAX AND MORITZ, Wilhelm Busch. Great children's classic, father of comic strip, of two bad boys, Max and Moritz. Also Ker and Plunk (Plisch und Plumm), Cat and Mouse, Deceitful Henry, Ice-Peter, The Boy and the Pipe, and five other pieces. Original German, with English translation. Edited by H. Arthur Klein; translations by various hands and H. Arthur Klein. vi + 216pp.
20181-3 Paperbound $1.50

PIGS IS PIGS AND OTHER FAVORITES, Ellis Parker Butler. The title story is one of the best humor short stories, as Mike Flannery obfuscates biology and English. Also included, That Pup of Murchison's, The Great American Pie Company, and Perkins of Portland. 14 illustrations. v + 109pp. 21532-6 Paperbound $1.00

THE PETERKIN PAPERS, Lucretia P. Hale. It takes genius to be as stupidly mad as the Peterkins, as they decide to become wise, celebrate the "Fourth," keep a cow, and otherwise strain the resources of the Lady from Philadelphia. Basic book of American humor. 153 illustrations. 219pp. 20794-3 Paperbound $1.25

PERRAULT'S FAIRY TALES, translated by A. E. Johnson and S. R. Littlewood, with 34 full-page illustrations by Gustave Doré. All the original Perrault stories—Cinderella, Sleeping Beauty, Bluebeard, Little Red Riding Hood, Puss in Boots, Tom Thumb, etc.—with their witty verse morals and the magnificent illustrations of Doré. One of the five or six great books of European fairy tales. viii + 117pp. 8⅛ x 11. 22311-6 Paperbound $2.00

OLD HUNGARIAN FAIRY TALES, Baroness Orczy. Favorites translated and adapted by author of the *Scarlet Pimpernel.* Eight fairy tales include "The Suitors of Princess Fire-Fly," "The Twin Hunchbacks," "Mr. Cuttlefish's Love Story," and "The Enchanted Cat." This little volume of magic and adventure will captivate children as it has for generations. 90 drawings by Montagu Barstow. 96pp.
(USO) 22293-4 Paperbound $1.95

TWO LITTLE SAVAGES; BEING THE ADVENTURES OF TWO BOYS WHO LIVED AS INDIANS AND WHAT THEY LEARNED, Ernest Thompson Seton. Great classic of nature and boyhood provides a vast range of woodlore in most palatable form, a genuinely entertaining story. Two farm boys build a teepee in woods and live in it for a month, working out Indian solutions to living problems, star lore, birds and animals, plants, etc. 293 illustrations. vii + 286pp.

20985-7 Paperbound $1.95

PETER PIPER'S PRACTICAL PRINCIPLES OF PLAIN & PERFECT PRONUNCIATION. Alliterative jingles and tongue-twisters of surprising charm, that made their first appearance in America about 1830. Republished in full with the spirited woodcut illustrations from this earliest American edition. 32pp. 4½ x 6⅜.

22560-7 Paperbound $1.00

SCIENCE EXPERIMENTS AND AMUSEMENTS FOR CHILDREN, Charles Vivian. 73 easy experiments, requiring only materials found at home or easily available, such as candles, coins, steel wool, etc.; illustrate basic phenomena like vacuum, simple chemical reaction, etc. All safe. Modern, well-planned. Formerly *Science Games for Children*. 102 photos, numerous drawings. 96pp. 6⅛ x 9¼.

21856-2 Paperbound $1.25

AN INTRODUCTION TO CHESS MOVES AND TACTICS SIMPLY EXPLAINED, Leonard Barden. Informal intermediate introduction, quite strong in explaining reasons for moves. Covers basic material, tactics, important openings, traps, positional play in middle game, end game. Attempts to isolate patterns and recurrent configurations. Formerly *Chess*. 58 figures. 102pp. (USO) 21210-6 Paperbound $1.25

LASKER'S MANUAL OF CHESS, Dr. Emanuel Lasker. Lasker was not only one of the five great World Champions, he was also one of the ablest expositors, theorists, and analysts. In many ways, his Manual, permeated with his philosophy of battle, filled with keen insights, is one of the greatest works ever written on chess. Filled with analyzed games by the great players. A single-volume library that will profit almost any chess player, beginner or master. 308 diagrams. xli x 349pp.

20640-8 Paperbound $2.50

THE MASTER BOOK OF MATHEMATICAL RECREATIONS, Fred Schuh. In opinion of many the finest work ever prepared on mathematical puzzles, stunts, recreations; exhaustively thorough explanations of mathematics involved, analysis of effects, citation of puzzles and games. Mathematics involved is elementary. Translated by F. Göbel. 194 figures. xxiv + 430pp.

22134-2 Paperbound $3.00

MATHEMATICS, MAGIC AND MYSTERY, Martin Gardner. Puzzle editor for Scientific American explains mathematics behind various mystifying tricks: card tricks, stage "mind reading," coin and match tricks, counting out games, geometric dissections, etc. Probability sets, theory of numbers clearly explained. Also provides more than 400 tricks, guaranteed to work, that you can do. 135 illustrations. xii + 176pp.

20338-2 Paperbound $1.50

"ESSENTIAL GRAMMAR" SERIES

All you really need to know about modern, colloquial grammar. Many educational shortcuts help you learn faster, understand better. Detailed cognate lists teach you to recognize similarities between English and foreign words and roots—make learning vocabulary easy and interesting. Excellent for independent study or as a supplement to record courses.

ESSENTIAL FRENCH GRAMMAR, Seymour Resnick. 2500-item cognate list. 159pp.
(EBE) 20419-7 Paperbound $1.25

ESSENTIAL GERMAN GRAMMAR, Guy Stern and Everett F. Bleiler. Unusual short-cuts on noun declension, word order, compound verbs. 124pp.
(EBE) 20422-7 Paperbound $1.25

ESSENTIAL ITALIAN GRAMMAR, Olga Ragusa. 111pp.
(EBE) 20779-X Paperbound $1.25

ESSENTIAL JAPANESE GRAMMAR, Everett F. Bleiler. In Romaji transcription; no characters needed. Japanese grammar is regular and simple. 156pp.
21027-8 Paperbound $1.25

ESSENTIAL PORTUGUESE GRAMMAR, Alexander da R. Prista. vi + 114pp.
21650-0 Paperbound $1.25

ESSENTIAL SPANISH GRAMMAR, Seymour Resnick. 2500 word cognate list. 115pp.
(EBE) 20780-3 Paperbound $1.25

ESSENTIAL ENGLISH GRAMMAR, Philip Gucker. Combines best features of modern, functional and traditional approaches. For refresher, class use, home study. x + 177pp.
21649-7 Paperbound $1.25

A PHRASE AND SENTENCE DICTIONARY OF SPOKEN SPANISH. Prepared for U. S. War Department by U. S. linguists. As above, unit is idiom, phrase or sentence rather than word. English-Spanish and Spanish-English sections contain modern equivalents of over 18,000 sentences. Introduction and appendix as above. iv + 513pp.
20495-2 Paperbound $2.00

A PHRASE AND SENTENCE DICTIONARY OF SPOKEN RUSSIAN. Dictionary prepared for U. S. War Department by U. S. linguists. Basic unit is not the word, but the idiom, phrase or sentence. English-Russian and Russian-English sections contain modern equivalents for over 30,000 phrases. Grammatical introduction covers phonetics, writing, syntax. Appendix of word lists for food, numbers, geographical names, etc. vi + 573 pp. 6⅛ x 9¼.
20496-0 Paperbound $3.00

CONVERSATIONAL CHINESE FOR BEGINNERS, Morris Swadesh. Phonetic system, beginner's course in Pai Hua Mandarin Chinese covering most important, most useful speech patterns. Emphasis on modern colloquial usage. Formerly *Chinese in Your Pocket*. xvi + 158pp.
21123-1 Paperbound $1.50

How to Know the Wild Flowers, Mrs. William Starr Dana. This is the classical book of American wildflowers (of the Eastern and Central United States), used by hundreds of thousands. Covers over 500 species, arranged in extremely easy to use color and season groups. Full descriptions, much plant lore. This Dover edition is the fullest ever compiled, with tables of nomenclature changes. 174 full-page plates by M. Satterlee. xii + 418pp. 20332-8 Paperbound $2.50

Our Plant Friends and Foes, William Atherton DuPuy. History, economic importance, essential botanical information and peculiarities of 25 common forms of plant life are provided in this book in an entertaining and charming style. Covers food plants (potatoes, apples, beans, wheat, almonds, bananas, etc.), flowers (lily, tulip, etc.), trees (pine, oak, elm, etc.), weeds, poisonous mushrooms and vines, gourds, citrus fruits, cotton, the cactus family, and much more. 108 illustrations. xiv + 290pp. 22272-1 Paperbound $2.00

How to Know the Ferns, Frances T. Parsons. Classic survey of Eastern and Central ferns, arranged according to clear, simple identification key. Excellent introduction to greatly neglected nature area. 57 illustrations and 42 plates. xvi + 215pp. 20740-4 Paperbound $1.75

Manual of the Trees of North America, Charles S. Sargent. America's foremost dendrologist provides the definitive coverage of North American trees and tree-like shrubs. 717 species fully described and illustrated: exact distribution, down to township; full botanical description; economic importance; description of subspecies and races; habitat, growth data; similar material. Necessary to every serious student of tree-life. Nomenclature revised to present. Over 100 locating keys. 783 illustrations. lii + 934pp. 20277-1, 20278-X Two volumes, Paperbound $6.00

Our Northern Shrubs, Harriet L. Keeler. Fine non-technical reference work identifying more than 225 important shrubs of Eastern and Central United States and Canada. Full text covering botanical description, habitat, plant lore, is paralleled with 205 full-page photographs of flowering or fruiting plants. Nomenclature revised by Edward G. Voss. One of few works concerned with shrubs. 205 plates, 35 drawings. xxviii + 521pp. 21989-5 Paperbound $3.75

The Mushroom Handbook, Louis C. C. Krieger. Still the best popular handbook: full descriptions of 259 species, cross references to another 200. Extremely thorough text enables you to identify, know all about any mushroom you are likely to meet in eastern and central U. S. A.: habitat, luminescence, poisonous qualities, use, folklore, etc. 32 color plates show over 50 mushrooms, also 126 other illustrations. Finding keys. vii + 560pp. 21861-9 Paperbound $3.95

Handbook of Birds of Eastern North America, Frank M. Chapman. Still much the best single-volume guide to the birds of Eastern and Central United States. Very full coverage of 675 species, with descriptions, life habits, distribution, similar data. All descriptions keyed to two-page color chart. With this single volume the average birdwatcher needs no other books. 1931 revised edition. 195 illustrations. xxxvi + 581pp. 21489-3 Paperbound $3.25

AMERICAN FOOD AND GAME FISHES, David S. Jordan and Barton W. Evermann. Definitive source of information, detailed and accurate enough to enable the sportsman and nature lover to identify conclusively some 1,000 species and sub-species of North American fish, sought for food or sport. Coverage of range, physiology, habits, life history, food value. Best methods of capture, interest to the angler, advice on bait, fly-fishing, etc. 338 drawings and photographs. 1 + 574pp. 6⅝ x 9⅜.
22383-1 Paperbound $4.50

THE FROG BOOK, Mary C. Dickerson. Complete with extensive finding keys, over 300 photographs, and an introduction to the general biology of frogs and toads, this is the classic non-technical study of Northeastern and Central species. 58 species; 290 photographs and 16 color plates. xvii + 253pp.
21973-9 Paperbound $4.00

THE MOTH BOOK: A GUIDE TO THE MOTHS OF NORTH AMERICA, William J. Holland. Classical study, eagerly sought after and used for the past 60 years. Clear identification manual to more than 2,000 different moths, largest manual in existence. General information about moths, capturing, mounting, classifying, etc., followed by species by species descriptions. 263 illustrations plus 48 color plates show almost every species, full size. 1968 edition, preface, nomenclature changes by A. E. Brower. xxiv + 479pp. of text. 6½ x 9¼.
21948-8 Paperbound $5.00

THE SEA-BEACH AT EBB-TIDE, Augusta Foote Arnold. Interested amateur can identify hundreds of marine plants and animals on coasts of North America; marine algae; seaweeds; squids; hermit crabs; horse shoe crabs; shrimps; corals; sea anemones; etc. Species descriptions cover: structure; food; reproductive cycle; size; shape; color; habitat; etc. Over 600 drawings. 85 plates. xii + 490pp.
21949-6 Paperbound $3.50

COMMON BIRD SONGS, Donald J. Borror. 33⅓ 12-inch record presents songs of 60 important birds of the eastern United States. A thorough, serious record which provides several examples for each bird, showing different types of song, individual variations, etc. Inestimable identification aid for birdwatcher. 32-page booklet gives text about birds and songs, with illustration for each bird.
21829-5 Record, book, album. Monaural. $2.75

FADS AND FALLACIES IN THE NAME OF SCIENCE, Martin Gardner. Fair, witty appraisal of cranks and quacks of science: Atlantis, Lemuria, hollow earth, flat earth, Velikovsky, orgone energy, Dianetics, flying saucers, Bridey Murphy, food fads, medical fads, perpetual motion, etc. Formerly "In the Name of Science." x + 363pp.
20394-8 Paperbound $2.00

HOAXES, Curtis D. MacDougall. Exhaustive, unbelievably rich account of great hoaxes: Locke's moon hoax, Shakespearean forgeries, sea serpents, Loch Ness monster, Cardiff giant, John Wilkes Booth's mummy, Disumbrationist school of art, dozens more; also journalism, psychology of hoaxing. 54 illustrations. xi + 338pp.
20465-0 Paperbound $2.75

CATALOGUE OF DOVER BOOKS

THE PRINCIPLES OF PSYCHOLOGY, William James. The famous long course, complete and unabridged. Stream of thought, time perception, memory, experimental methods—these are only some of the concerns of a work that was years ahead of its time and still valid, interesting, useful. 94 figures. Total of xviii + 1391pp.
20381-6, 20382-4 Two volumes, Paperbound $6.00

THE STRANGE STORY OF THE QUANTUM, Banesh Hoffmann. Non-mathematical but thorough explanation of work of Planck, Einstein, Bohr, Pauli, de Broglie, Schrödinger, Heisenberg, Dirac, Feynman, etc. No technical background needed. "Of books attempting such an account, this is the best," Henry Margenau, Yale. 40-page "Postscript 1959." xii + 285pp.
20518-5 Paperbound $2.00

THE RISE OF THE NEW PHYSICS, A. d'Abro. Most thorough explanation in print of central core of mathematical physics, both classical and modern; from Newton to Dirac and Heisenberg. Both history and exposition; philosophy of science, causality, explanations of higher mathematics, analytical mechanics, electromagnetism, thermodynamics, phase rule, special and general relativity, matrices. No higher mathematics needed to follow exposition, though treatment is elementary to intermediate in level. Recommended to serious student who wishes verbal understanding. 97 illustrations. xvii + 982pp.
20003-5, 20004-3 Two volumes, Paperbound $5.50

GREAT IDEAS OF OPERATIONS RESEARCH, Jagjit Singh. Easily followed non-technical explanation of mathematical tools, aims, results: statistics, linear programming, game theory, queueing theory, Monte Carlo simulation, etc. Uses only elementary mathematics. Many case studies, several analyzed in detail. Clarity, breadth make this excellent for specialist in another field who wishes background. 41 figures. x + 228pp.
21886-4 Paperbound $2.25

GREAT IDEAS OF MODERN MATHEMATICS: THEIR NATURE AND USE, Jagjit Singh. Internationally famous expositor, winner of Unesco's Kalinga Award for science popularization explains verbally such topics as differential equations, matrices, groups, sets, transformations, mathematical logic and other important modern mathematics, as well as use in physics, astrophysics, and similar fields. Superb exposition for layman, scientist in other areas. viii + 312pp.
20587-8 Paperbound $2.25

GREAT IDEAS IN INFORMATION THEORY, LANGUAGE AND CYBERNETICS, Jagjit Singh. The analog and digital computers, how they work, how they are like and unlike the human brain, the men who developed them, their future applications, computer terminology. An essential book for today, even for readers with little math. Some mathematical demonstrations included for more advanced readers. 118 figures. Tables. ix + 338pp.
21694-2 Paperbound $2.25

CHANCE, LUCK AND STATISTICS, Horace C. Levinson. Non-mathematical presentation of fundamentals of probability theory and science of statistics and their applications. Games of chance, betting odds, misuse of statistics, normal and skew distributions, birth rates, stock speculation, insurance. Enlarged edition. Formerly "The Science of Chance." xiii + 357pp.
21007-3 Paperbound $2.00

CATALOGUE OF DOVER BOOKS

THE PHILOSOPHY OF THE UPANISHADS, Paul Deussen. Clear, detailed statement of upanishadic system of thought, generally considered among best available. History of these works, full exposition of system emergent from them, parallel concepts in the West. Translated by A. S. Geden. xiv + 429pp.
21616-0 Paperbound $3.00

LANGUAGE, TRUTH AND LOGIC, Alfred J. Ayer. Famous, remarkably clear introduction to the Vienna and Cambridge schools of Logical Positivism; function of philosophy, elimination of metaphysical thought, nature of analysis, similar topics. "Wish I had written it myself," Bertrand Russell. 2nd, 1946 edition. 160pp.
20010-8 Paperbound $1.35

THE GUIDE FOR THE PERPLEXED, Moses Maimonides. Great classic of medieval Judaism, major attempt to reconcile revealed religion (Pentateuch, commentaries) and Aristotelian philosophy. Enormously important in all Western thought. Unabridged Friedländer translation. 50-page introduction. lix + 414pp.
(USO) 20351-4 Paperbound $2.50

OCCULT AND SUPERNATURAL PHENOMENA, D. H. Rawcliffe. Full, serious study of the most persistent delusions of mankind: crystal gazing, mediumistic trance, stigmata, lycanthropy, fire walking, dowsing, telepathy, ghosts, ESP, etc., and their relation to common forms of abnormal psychology. Formerly *Illusions and Delusions of the Supernatural and the Occult.* iii + 551pp.   20503-7 Paperbound $3.50

THE EGYPTIAN BOOK OF THE DEAD: THE PAPYRUS OF ANI, E. A. Wallis Budge. Full hieroglyphic text, interlinear transliteration of sounds, word for word translation, then smooth, connected translation; Theban recension. Basic work in Ancient Egyptian civilization; now even more significant than ever for historical importance, dilation of consciousness, etc. clvi + 377pp. 6½ x 9¼.
21866-X Paperbound $3.75

PSYCHOLOGY OF MUSIC, Carl E. Seashore. Basic, thorough survey of everything known about psychology of music up to 1940's; essential reading for psychologists, musicologists. Physical acoustics; auditory apparatus; relationship of physical sound to perceived sound; role of the mind in sorting, altering, suppressing, creating sound sensations; musical learning, testing for ability, absolute pitch, other topics. Records of Caruso, Menuhin analyzed. 88 figures. xix + 408pp.
21851-1 Paperbound $2.75

THE I CHING (THE BOOK OF CHANGES), translated by James Legge. Complete translated text plus appendices by Confucius, of perhaps the most penetrating divination book ever compiled. Indispensable to all study of early Oriental civilizations. 3 plates. xxiii + 448pp.   21062-6 Paperbound $2.75

THE UPANISHADS, translated by Max Müller. Twelve classical upanishads: Chandogya, Kena, Aitareya, Kaushitaki, Isa, Katha, Mundaka, Taittiriyaka, Brhadaranyaka, Svetasvatara, Prasna, Maitriyana. 160-page introduction, analysis by Prof. Müller. Total of 826pp.   20398-0, 20399-9 Two volumes, Paperbound $5.00

CATALOGUE OF DOVER BOOKS

MATHEMATICAL PUZZLES FOR BEGINNERS AND ENTHUSIASTS, Geoffrey Mott-Smith. 189 puzzles from easy to difficult—involving arithmetic, logic, algebra, properties of digits, probability, etc.—for enjoyment and mental stimulus. Explanation of mathematical principles behind the puzzles. 135 illustrations. viii + 248pp.
20198-8 Paperbound $1.25

PAPER FOLDING FOR BEGINNERS, William D. Murray and Francis J. Rigney. Easiest book on the market, clearest instructions on making interesting, beautiful origami. Sail boats, cups, roosters, frogs that move legs, bonbon boxes, standing birds, etc. 40 projects; more than 275 diagrams and photographs. 94pp.
20713-7 Paperbound $1.00

TRICKS AND GAMES ON THE POOL TABLE, Fred Herrmann. 79 tricks and games—some solitaires, some for two or more players, some competitive games—to entertain you between formal games. Mystifying shots and throws, unusual caroms, tricks involving such props as cork, coins, a hat, etc. Formerly *Fun on the Pool Table*. 77 figures. 95pp.
21814-7 Paperbound $1.00

HAND SHADOWS TO BE THROWN UPON THE WALL: A SERIES OF NOVEL AND AMUSING FIGURES FORMED BY THE HAND, Henry Bursill. Delightful picturebook from great-grandfather's day shows how to make 18 different hand shadows: a bird that flies, duck that quacks, dog that wags his tail, camel, goose, deer, boy, turtle, etc. Only book of its sort. vi + 33pp. 6½ x 9¼. 21779-5 Paperbound $1.00

WHITTLING AND WOODCARVING, E. J. Tangerman. 18th printing of best book on market. "If you can cut a potato you can carve" toys and puzzles, chains, chessmen, caricatures, masks, frames, woodcut blocks, surface patterns, much more. Information on tools, woods, techniques. Also goes into serious wood sculpture from Middle Ages to present, East and West. 464 photos, figures. x + 293pp.
20965-2 Paperbound $2.00

HISTORY OF PHILOSOPHY, Julián Marias. Possibly the clearest, most easily followed, best planned, most useful one-volume history of philosophy on the market; neither skimpy nor overfull. Full details on system of every major philosopher and dozens of less important thinkers from pre-Socratics up to Existentialism and later. Strong on many European figures usually omitted. Has gone through dozens of editions in Europe. 1966 edition, translated by Stanley Appelbaum and Clarence Strowbridge. xviii + 505pp.
21739-6 Paperbound $3.00

YOGA: A SCIENTIFIC EVALUATION, Kovoor T. Behanan. Scientific but non-technical study of physiological results of yoga exercises; done under auspices of Yale U. Relations to Indian thought, to psychoanalysis, etc. 16 photos. xxiii + 270pp.
20505-3 Paperbound $2.50

Prices subject to change without notice.
Available at your book dealer or write for free catalogue to Dept. GI, Dover Publications, Inc., 180 Varick St., N. Y., N. Y. 10014. Dover publishes more than 150 books each year on science, elementary and advanced mathematics, biology, music, art, literary history, social sciences and other areas.

739.533   741650

Michaelis
   Antique pewter of the British
   Isles.

OCT 10	DATE DUE	
MAY 05		